LESSONS from the
NORDSTROM
WAY

LESSONS from the

NORDSTROM

WAY

How Companies Are Emulating the
#1 CUSTOMER SERVICE
COMPANY

ROBERT SPECTOR

John Wiley & Sons, Inc.

New York • Chichester • Weinheim • Brisbane • Singapore • Toronto

This book is printed on acid-free paper. ∞

Copyright © 2001 by Robert Spector. All rights reserved.

Published by John Wiley & Sons, Inc.
Published simultaneously in Canada.

This publication is designed to provide accurate and authoritative information in regard to the subject matter covered. It is sold with the understanding that the publisher is not engaged in rendering legal, accounting, or other professional services. If legal advice or other expert assistance is required, the services of a competent professional person should be sought.

Library of Congress Cataloging-in-Publication Data:

Spector, Robert, 1947–
    Lessons from the Nordstrom way : how companies are
    emulating the #1 customer service company / Robert Spector.
      p. cm.
    ISBN 0-471-35594-1 (cloth : alk. paper)
    1. Customer services—United States.
    HF5415.5 .S6267 2000   00-043589

Printed in the United States of America.

10 9 8 7 6 5 4 3 2 1

To the memory of
James F. "Jim" Nordstrom.
And for all the companies who strive to be
the Nordstrom of their industry.

Preface

For almost a century, Nordstrom has distinguished itself from the competition when it comes to customer service. When *The Nordstrom Way* was first published in 1995, it struck a chord with many companies, in a variety of industries. Almost 100,000 copies and a second edition later, it continues to serve as an inspiration and a guide for many different types of businesses. In the fall of 1996, it became clear to me that many executives and managers that had read *The Nordstrom Way* or attended one of my presentations, had begun putting some of Nordstrom's most valuable lessons to practice in their own companies. When placed in new contexts, those lessons were expanded and built upon. *Lessons from the Nordstrom Way* is derived from the application of *The Nordstrom Way* and is meant to share the real life business stories that prove its effectiveness. I had the pleasure of hearing those stories firsthand from the principals of the companies profiled in this new book, whose words on a variety of customer service issues you'll hear.

The first inspiration for this book came from John Cochran, chairman and chief executive officer of First Merit Bank Corp., and his team. In the fall of 1996,

Cochran was in the midst of recreating the company to make it more responsive to the customer. His goal, he would later tell me, was to "Empower employees to use customer service as a means to grow the business niche very fast." But what he lacked was a clear way to make it happen. To help find a method, Cochran bought 100 copies of *The Nordstrom Way* for his top executives, and then took the 22-person executive team on a corporate retreat to discuss how they were going to become a company known for quality customer service. Eight managers were assigned to each of the chapters of the book and to lead a discussion about it at the retreat.

"We found that Nordstrom is very well defined as to what the company is, and what it isn't," says Cochran. "We decided that we should clearly define the FirstMerit way so that it empowers our people to act in the best interests of the company, without a lot of rules and regulations—naturally just like Nordstrom." After the retreat, Cochran sent me the results, which consisted of a dozen 8½" x 11" sheets of paper with column headings that read "The Nordstrom Way" on one half of the page and "The FirstMerit Way" on the other half. Under "The Nordstrom Way" were the key principles that Nordstrom follows. Under "The FirstMerit Way" were the ways the bank reinterpreted and tailored those principles for its own business.

The moment I saw what the people at FirstMerit had done, I knew that it could be the basis of an important book. Many companies want to be the Nordstrom of their industry—yet they don't really have an understanding of how to begin the process. *The Nordstrom Way* offered the gestalt of the company's customer service philosophy, but it didn't provide a step-by-step approach. That's the purpose of *Lessons from the Nordstrom Way*. By following the eight Nordstrom management principles identified here, companies can now systematically become the Nordstrom of their industry.

The firms profiled in this new book are very different from one another—and represent both large and small businesses across a variety of industries. I found the companies used as examples in several ways—both deliberately and coincidentally. The W Hotel brand is included because I stayed at the W New York on Lexington Avenue and was immediately impressed by the commitment to customer service; I later found out the chain has long followed Nordstrom's principles. Continental Airlines is a carrier I've long admired for their customer service principles, as well. The Feed the Children charitable organization was suggested by Mark Victor Hansen, co-author of *Chicken Soup for the Soul*, with whom I was autographing books at a conference of Meeting Professionals International, the same place where I met Terri Breining of Concepts Worldwide, a meeting planning company with a customer service focus. Roy Williams, author of *The Wizard of Ads*, told me about Mike's Carwash and Kessler's Diamond Center. I thought it important to include some family businesses in the mix. I discovered St. Charles Medical Center while I was researching a speech for the American Society of Hospital Engineering, and USinternetworking (USi) from an article in *Fortune* magazine. (I later learned that John Tomljanovic, USi's Vice President of Client Care gives a copy of *The Nordstrom Way* to every new employee.) Callison Architecture has had a close association with Nordstrom for three decades; the company has designed most of the stores in the chain. Brooke White, the head of Nordstrom's public relations told me about Fafie Moore of Realty Executives of Nevada, who is truly a student of Nordstrom.

I purposely chose an eclectic group of firms to show how these principles apply to every type of company that feels that customer service is essential to its success. If you are a company that sincerely wants to become the Nordstrom of your industry, no matter what that industry is, this book provides a blueprint for how to do it.

ROBERT SPECTOR

Acknowledgments

This book could not have been written without the support and encouragement of many people.

An extra special salute to John Cochran and the people at FirstMerit Corporation for inspiring the idea for this book.

Many thanks to Gordon Bethune of Continental Airlines; Fafie and Jeff Moore of Realty Executives of Nevada; Christopher McLeary and John Tomljanovic of USinternetworking; James T. Lussier of St. Charles Medical Center; Guy Hensley, Thomas Martin, Al Petrone, and Thomas Limberg of W Hotels; Robert J. Tindall, John Bierly, Stan Laegreid, and M.J. Munsell of Callison Architecture, Inc.; Theresa Breining of Concepts Worldwide; William, Jerry, and Mike Dahm of Mike's Carwashes, Inc.; Paul Bigham of Feed the Children; and Richard Kessler of Kessler's Diamond Center.

Also, thanks to Charles Catapano, Kimberly Elek, Carol Frey, Julie Gardner, Lissa Gruman, Patrick J. McCarthy, Gail McQuary, George Paidas, Brenda Perry, Renata Maria Schweiger, Ilene Shapiro, Roy Williams, and Laura Worthington.

Much appreciation to Ruth Mills for championing this project at John Wiley & Sons, Inc., and Airié Dekidjiev, for her insightful editing.

As always, I am indebted to my agent, Elizabeth Wales, and to Nancy Shawn of Wales Literary Agency.

And finally, my love, affection, and appreciation to my wife, Marybeth, and my daughter, Fae.

R.S.

Contents

1 Provide Your Customers with Choices

How do I love thee? Let me count the ways.
—Robert Browning

Most of us want choices, and plenty of them. The unabashed consumers among us in particular relish the thought of being presented with lots of options, whether we are shopping for shoes or checking into a hotel (even a hospital). The same desire for variety plays itself out in many forms. If you're running a business, you want to know what your software applications service provider furnishes that its competition does not. The more choices you offer your customers, the more likely they will do business with you, rather than your competition.

At Nordstrom, one of the ways *choice* is secured is by stocking stores with wide and deep inventories of merchandise—shoes, apparel, and cosmetics from a broad cross section of manufacturers. From its origins in 1901 as a modest shoe store to its present form, Nordstrom has always believed that if you offer your customer length and breadth and depth of merchandise, the less likely she will walk out of the store without making a purchase—or two or three.

A typical Nordstrom store carries upwards of 150,000 pairs of shoes, with the world's widest selection of sizes and widths—from 2½ to 14, AAAAAA to E for women, and 5 to 18, AAA to EEE for men—in a broad range of styles and colors. Unlike much of the competition, the store carries many half sizes. My wife's shoe size is 10½ narrow; she can buy her shoes only at Nordstrom.

Nordstrom has extended the philosophy of providing a wealth of choices to its Web businesses: nordstrom.com and nordstromshoes.com. The latter offers over 20 million pairs of shoes. Nordstrom also reinforces the importance of offering choices in its advertising strategy. One recent ad shows four distinctly different looking men having a business meeting. One man is tall, another is short; one is stocky, another thin. The headline reads: "Every man deserves a great looking, great fitting suit."

The idea of choice also extends to other facilities in the store. A typical Nordstrom store offers its customers the option of choosing from four different kinds of restaurants. An espresso bar located at an entrance outside the store offers gourmet coffee drinks, Italian sodas, and pastries and cookies to Nordstrom customers as well as people walking through the mall. Café Nordstrom serves soups, salads, sandwiches, and beverages in a cafeteria format, offering a lower priced alternative. The Garden Court offers full-service dining with fresh, seasonal produce and seafood in an elegant atmosphere. The Pub is a clubby dining area that serves coffee and breakfast items from 9:30 to 11:30 AM and sandwiches, salads, cocktails, stouts, and ales the rest of the day.

The Pub, which is strategically located adjacent to the men's suits department, has turned into such a popular lunch spot that it is sometimes difficult to get a table. In the event a customer has to wait a while before being seated, Nordstrom doesn't want that precious customer heading out the door to look for an alternative; after all, in a shopping mall or the busy downtown area of a city, the customer has many, many choices of where to eat. To ensure that the customer stays, Nordstrom gives her a beeper to continue to shop throughout the store; she will be beeped when her table is ready. In short, Nordstrom wants to wrap its collective arms around its customers and never let them go. A multitude of choices make those arms stretch a little bit farther.

When it comes to choices, Costco, Inc., the chain of 148,000-square-foot warehouse "stores," takes a different approach to customer service, but is met with the same result. "We thought that a great deal of what was going on in retail added up to a bad customer service experience," said Costco chairman Jeff Brotman. "We told the retail customer: We will not be providing salespeople or locations as convenient as you can get at Nordstrom; we won't be providing the fixturing, delivery, the billing, or a vast selection of mayonnaise or tissues. But what we are going to do is narrow down the product assortment and cut down the self-select process for you. We're going to eliminate costs, and we're going to give you the benefit of the cost reduction. And then we're going to try to make it easy to get in and to get out. When asked to rate our customer service, customers rate it very, very high—and we have none, in the traditional sense. The service to the customer that we provide is the best value possible in each product. We have only 3,500 products. We think about every product that we sell. The metaphor for the value you get inside Costco is our hot dog and soda for a $1.50. The subtleties of what we do are not lost on the customer, but they are lost on the pundits." This is proof that a focus on choice is crucial, but how you approach the issue of offering choices should be customized to your business. You must ask yourself: What kind of choices do you offer your customers? And if you think you are offering them plenty of choices, do you think that's enough?

FirstMerit Bancorporation: Establish a Cultlike Devotion to Selling

At FirstMerit Corporation, a bank based in Akron, Ohio, providing customers with choices is an essential part of doing business in the highly competitive world of personal finance. The bank, which has close to $10 billion in assets, has been growing at a rapid pace for a variety of reasons, one of which is what *American Banker* has called a "cultlike devotion to selling."

For the individual account, FirstMerit offers the typical 24/7 type of banking options: strategically located branches, Internet services, and ATM machines for easy access and telephone services. Customers are also given choices of distribution channels. John Cochran, who has been chairman and chief executive officer of First-Merit since 1995 explains:

> *They can do their business when, how, and where they want to. That means that they can use an ATM, the Internet, a branch, or a telephone to do their business. That way, they can define convenience in their own manner. With that, we want to add the relationship delivery and high quality service that are not distinctive of larger institutions.*

It is primarily in the realm of business banking that FirstMerit offers a full range of choices that reach beyond convention. The core of FirstMerit's customer base is some 25,000 small and medium-sized businesses in the very concentrated northeast Ohio marketplace. FirstMerit services about 40 percent of that market share in its territory through 177 branches. These customers need the same wide array of banking options that much larger businesses require.

"Breadth and depth of your product line is very important," said Cochran. "We are considered a smaller institution, but we're also a relationship institution so we need to have a broad product line that can compete with the big guys. We want to make sure customers do not have to compromise when they choose to do their business with us. We don't compromise the product line choices. They get the same kind of capability of sophistication of product line that they get with the big guys." The product line for these small to medium-sized businesses consists of three different elements, which FirstMerit illustrates for customers with a symbolic triangle:

1. The first element of the triangle supports the business itself through a wide variety of products, including all types of credit, depository instruments, cash management services, pension and profit-sharing programs, and international banking services.

2. The second element of the triangle consists of private banking services for owners and managers. FirstMerit's private banking centers take care of personal banking needs such as purchasing a home, home equities, investing in education for the customers' children, estate planning, and dealing with stock options received from their company. "We have a special division

that deals with nothing but building and funding the benefits and the succession planning for the future management of that company," said Cochran. "If an owner wants to pass the business on to an offspring, we have a very sophisticated product line that deals with succession planning. The owner will be able to pay the estate taxes in that transfer and to make that ownership transferable with the least amount of tax liability."

3. The employees of the company represent the third part of the triangle. FirstMerit provide them with personal banking products such as checking accounts, home mortgages, and credit cards.

"We wanted to build a product line that meets all of the constituencies of a company: The company itself, its owners and managers, and the employees. It's the responsibility of the FirstMerit banker—and his or her team—to create the kind of a relationship with that customer account that will enable them to satisfy every one of those elements," said Cochran. The end result is that a strategy for offering choice is defined by the company's important consumers and tailor-made to their needs.

How does FirstMerit make sure that its wide variety of choices are offered to—and used by—consumers and that the company's long-term goals are accomplished? First of all, to help employees feel comfortable talking about those additional products, FirstMerit trains them to be well versed in everything a corporate customer might need. All of the employees involved in selling the various bank products are assembled as teams and are taught each other's business, which includes a broad and detailed explanation of the features and benefits of each product and service that a corporate customer would need. They are taught how to identify that need and how to speak to the benefits of that product. The building up of relationships among and between these employees creates camaraderie and a greater desire to help the group.

Just as important, FirstMerit business bankers—like any good salespeople—are trained in how to deal with customer resistance. First they're told which objections to expect from customers and then they're taught the best way to respond to those objections. They should also know when to smoothly and politely hand off the customer to the FirstMerit service provider who is trained to explain the product in greater detail. "It's important to build that proper protocol of referral," says Cochran. "It's equally important for the banker who receives the referral to acknowledge the employee who made it happen."

A frontline employee's initial contact with a small-business customer often begins with opening him or her a checking account and/or starting a line of credit. After that account is open, it's time for multiple selling. The employee tells the customer, that now that he's established a credit line, he will probably be requiring other group-banking services such as pension, profit-sharing, personal banking, international banking, or cash management. By introducing those products, FirstMerit hopes that these additional options will further attract the employees of the customer-company into the FirstMerit fold. Because their boss or the owner of the company banks with FirstMerit, those employees are eligible for some free services, too, a bonus added to solidify the deal. Says Cochran:

Our approach is similar to Nordstrom's. When some-one walks into the clothing department at Nordstrom and buys a suit he gets complete attention. The salesperson who sold the customer that suit then takes the customer into another department to sell him shirts and ties and socks. The responsibility of the person who opened that line of credit or checking account is to introduce the customer to the additional services.

The most essential component of providing customers with choices is paying attention to what the customer is saying. For example, a customer once told a FirstMerit customer service representative that he had just been awarded a large monetary claim from an insurance company for a personal injury. The FirstMerit customer service representative immediately referred the customer to FirstMerit's trust department, where an expert spoke to the customer about the necessity for estate planning. As a result of this emphasis on multiple selling, FirstMerit employees increased their rate of sales from less than one product a day in 1995 to nearly seven products a day in 1998.

FirstMerit employees don't educate themselves on every product their bank provides just so they can be altruistic team players. There's further incentive—in extra pay—involved in the deal as well. For all employees—from tellers to branch managers—who come in direct contact with customers, 20 percent of their compensation is tied directly to their ability to sell the customer on buying a product that they don't personally sell themselves. Each employee has a goal of a certain number of referrals that result in sales. Another goal is based on the total dollar value of those closed referrals.

For example, a business banker is responsible for building $10,000 worth of profitability for products sold by partners in her team. Let's say a particular trust was worth $1,000. If that business banker sent the customer to a trust officer and that trust officer sold the customer a pension plan with a first-year profitability of $1,000, that would count for $1,000 toward the $10,000 goal. Once the employee reaches that goal, it activates 20 percent of her compensation. Employees' sales transactions are tallied every week by a sophisticated $9 million computer platform system.

None of this success comes by accident. It's all part of a corporate strategy. Every January, FirstMerit hosts a three-day retreat called "Camp We Can Do," where 100 executives and managers—referred to as "coaches"— work on particular strategic goals. One year, for example, that goal was to increase the number of sales from referrals within the bank. On that retreat, employees were taught all the nuances of trust services and investment products by their coaches. To regularly remind coaches of the importance of referrals, they are all required to attend a one-day refresher retreat every quarter. If you're going to be offering the customer lots of choices, you've got to constantly educate yourself.

W Seattle Hotel: Make Your Customer Service Philosophy Whatever/Whenever

Created by Starwood Hotels and Resorts Worldwide, the parent company of Westin Hotels, W is a new concept in hotels. Although W is certainly not the most famous hotel brand in the world, it is included in this book because it is an especially customer-friendly service provider, with a mission of providing visitors with a completely satisfying consumer experience. I have stayed at the hotel many times and I still remember the first: The moment I stepped out of the taxi cab at the Lexington Avenue and 48th Street location, I was greeted by a friendly young man, dressed fashionably, in black, who served as my escort first to the front desk, and then to my room. There, he went into detail about all of the interesting details of my room, from the personal CD player to the comfortable mattress.

W Seattle was the fourth hotel built by the brand, preceded by units in New York, Atlanta, and San Francisco. Coincidentally, another company featured in this book, Callison Architecture, designed W Seattle, which opened in September 1999. It's important to note that customer-service-oriented companies are more likely to do business with similar minded companies.

As Tom Limberg, a veteran hotelier, who is general manager of W Seattle, said,

> *We've charged ourselves with the responsibility of being someone's home away from home, but with virtually no knowledge of what that home is all about. Consequently, we have to have the ability to provide choices and offer alternatives. Sometimes a customer wants something that we can't provide. Maybe it's not available. Maybe it's something we don't do. Our philosophy is to stay away from the "N" word ("No"). We hate the "N" word.*

Of course, the brand would never do anything illegal, but there are many ways to make a customer feel that he or she is being taken seriously. Providing alternatives—choices—is the best way to stay away from saying "No" to the customer. If you can't provide A, perhaps you can provide B. "For example," said Limberg, "Every room in our hotel comes with a Sony CD stereo player and a videocassette player—in the event that you don't like the movie that our in-house service provides. If you called down to the desk and wanted a movie that we didn't have, we would most likely go out and get you one at a local video store. That type of request is directed to W Hotel's customer service department, which is called Whatever/Whenever. That is our service mentality. That's what they do," explained Limberg.

The first week W Seattle was opened, a guest wanted to plug his laptop into the in-room high-speed Internet access port at the desktop. One problem: He had forgotten to bring his Ethernet connector. "It was very frustrating for him," recalled Limberg. "It was very frustrating for us, too. Linc, who is our lead Welcome Ambassador (the equivalent to a bell captain), is very computer literate. He searched around and finally found an Ethernet connector on one of the laptops that we use in our purchasing department, and he brought it up to the guest's room. Not having that connector knocked purchasing out of the water for a few hours, but that was okay because it happened at the waning part of their day. Most importantly, we rallied for the customer and provided him with what he needed."

As happy as he was to find a solution, Limberg was just as pleased that an employee was comfortable going into the administrative offices to get some results. "Linc didn't feel like there was a skull and cross-bones on the front door of the administrative offices saying: 'Solve those problems up there; we're busy with paper work,' " said Limberg. As a result of that episode, the hotel is now creating "an inventory of things like that for Whatever/Whenever, so that in the future we can more easily facilitate those types of requests." A crucial lesson to

be learned from this story is that companies need to empower their employees, in order for them to be able to
employ superb customer service strategies. Communication between employees and a shared mission are
crucial components of empowerment.

W Seattle, which is on the corner of Fourth Avenue
and Seneca Street in the heart of downtown, has a total
of 426 rooms—250 of them come with king-size beds—
and two floor plans. One floor plan consists of 80
L-shaped units called the "Cool Corner Kings" (because
they occupy the corners of the building), which have
floor-to-ceiling windows, and dramatic entryways.
These popular rooms have been in high demand since
the hotel opened. The second floor plan has the identi-
cal view of downtown and Elliott Bay, but with a different window arrangement—instead of the floor-to-ceiling
windows, each room has a window seat.

"Our approach to room types is to maintain our inventory and know where we are on that inventory," said
Limberg. "If a customer makes a specific request and we
know that we're not going to be able to satisfy that request, the time to address that and to provide the best
alternative is when we take the reservation. I'm a big be-
liever in keeping the customers in the loop. Include them
in the decision. Give them the news—good, bad, or in-
different—as quickly as you have it. You can't put off
that decision. We don't want our guests to think for a
moment, a day, or a week between the reservation process and their actual arrival that they might be getting
something that they're not going to get." The important
moral here is be honest with the customer and she can't
be disappointed.

Limberg has found that customer complaints, such
as not getting the type of room that was requested,

frequently end up on his desk, and he's glad they do. He says,

> *I've always found that when you're in a conversation with the customer, it almost always boils down to this: "If somebody had just let me know, I could have made other plans." We need to be on the same page as our staff—we call them* cast members—*on how we treat the customers, so we're not going in different directions.*

In customer-service-oriented companies, consistency for the consumer is always important. When a customer does not get what she wants, Limberg believes that it is not necessary to fully explain why the company was not able to fulfill the request. Communication with a guest should be on a need-to-know basis, says Limberg:

> *Another source of our problems is that we sometimes tell customers more than they need to know. They don't need to know the drama or minutia or what's going on behind the scenes. There's supposed to be a little sizzle—a little magic—when you get here. They don't need to know exactly how we do it. They just need to be the recipient of that magic.*

Like Nordstrom, the W Seattle offers several different restaurant services. The sleek lobby bar, like the bar at the W New York, has quickly become a place to see and be seen. The main restaurant, Earth and Ocean, which was created by the Myriad Restaurant Group, was written up in *The Wall Street Journal* just a few weeks after it opened. The W Seattle is surrounded by excellent restaurants within easy walking distance, but the hotel wants to give customers the choice of staying comfortable and dry, rather than go out dining in that familiar Seattle rain. Extending services slightly beyond expectations goes a long way toward keeping the customer happy.

USinternetworking: Respond Fast and Not Just to Your E-Mail!

USinternetworking (USi) is a pioneering Application Service Provider (ASP) founded in 1998. ASPs have a profound impact on how companies employ their internal software systems. ASPs like USinternetworking rent out access to computer software and hardware to business clients, a service that includes providing access over the Internet.

Business-to-business client service in the technology industry has specific requirements.

In order to be able to explain how business-to-business client service in the technology industry works, it's important to understand the business more closely. USi procures master licenses to programs that corporations use to operate enterprise applications such as accounting, e-mail, e-commerce, e-procurement, and human resources, from software vendors such as Microsoft Corp., PeopleSoft Inc., Siebel Systems Inc., Lawson Software, Ariba, Inc., and BroadVision Inc. Clients pay USi a fixed monthly fee to run and manage the software programs. They are run on USi servers at several sites around the world. The customers tap in either through the Internet or over telephone lines that are specifically dedicated to the software programs. Because these systems are costly to acquire and difficult to install and maintain, USi was a much needed resource and was able to create a crucial niche service for a broad cross-section of small, medium, and large companies such as Hershey Foods Corp., Liberty Financial Cos., Knoll Pharmaceutical Company (BASF), stockbroker Legg Mason Inc., and Franklin Covey, the parent company for the organization of business self-help guru, Stephen Covey, author of *The 7 Habits of Highly Effective People*. To attract these high caliber clients, USi offers a suite of products that are tailored to fit individual clients' needs for managing finances, human resources, product lines, and electronic commerce for a variety of software platforms. Says John Tomljanovic, USi's Vice President of Client Care:

> *What the client gets depends on the need that they define. If a client wants a system that can handle accounts payable, accounts receivable, and general ledger information—then they will want one type of product. We will work with them and recommend the best solution, customizing to their requirements. We don't hand them an out of the box package. We work with the client to understand what their business processes are and what would make the most sense. Technically, accounting is accounting, but each company does it a little differently. The difference is dictated by their business processes.*

After the programs have been installed, USi gives its clients the option of contacting and coordinating with USi via e-mail, phone, fax, or dedicated Web sites. All of the applications that the company sells to clients are Internet-based, and therefore easily accessible anywhere in the world. "We want our clients to feel comfortable that they have any number of ways that they can reach us for assistance," emphasizes Tomljanovic.

USi's philosophy is that regardless of the number of communication choices that it gives to its clients, every call to USi must result in a successful resolution of a re-quest or service problem. We give our clients the option of calling us on the phone if they prefer hearing a human voice," said Tomljanovic. "But we also want them to feel comfortable sending us an e-mail and to know that we are going to work on their problem just as dili-gently as we would on a telephone call that comes into our help desk."

USi has mapped out detailed procedures for every one of the communications options—e-mail, phone, Web, or fax—that clients can use. "When we first started to look at how we wanted to structure things, we knew we didn't want to create a big help-desk pool of people that a client can call into via a single 800 number. In that scenario, anyone who is sitting at a desk can answer the phone and try to help the client," Tomljanovic told me. "We wanted to set it up so that on that first call, we could answer 90 percent of the questions that a client could have for us."

Consequently, USi took a different approach by cre-ating Client Assistance Teams—known throughout the company by the acronym CATs—which provide dedi-cated service to designated clients.

> *CATs are involved with the [implementation] process up front. At the very end of the [installation] life cycle, after our implementation teams have had the opportunity to customize the applications to fit into the client's business processes, CATs are trained to fully understand what's been done and will know how to service the client based on the client's unique application.*

An account manager is responsible for each CAT team, which consists of Client-Care Associates, who work for that account manager. Each CAT is dedicated to satisfying the service needs of from two to six different clients, depending on the magnitude and size of the customer and the specific applications and services for which they contract with USi. In the case of all businesses that offer complex services, the question of how to provide adequate follow-up service must be answered.

USinternetworking aims for a much more personal experience between client and provider than that of the usual help desk model. As Tomljanovic explains, "We want to get to a point where if the client calls in, they know the person they are talking to. They don't have to explain what their system does or what they are trying to do in the big picture because the members of that particular CAT team are familiar with that client's system and how it has been custom-implemented for that particular client along with the more general goals of the client."

In all businesses there exists the danger that by the time the right person is on the line with the client or customer, he or she has already been bounced around from one anonymous voice to another, and is already fuming. I'm sure you, gentle reader, can relate to a similar scenario. Every customer-service-oriented business must have a plan to make sure that doesn't happen.

When USi receives an e-mail from a client during business hours, it is the company policy to respond to the client within 20 minutes, letting the client know that the e-mail has been received and that the company is dealing with the nature of the correspondence. Not only does the USinternetworking client receive personal care, but also he receives the assurance of a timely response, no matter which method of communication the client chose.

St. Charles Medical Center: Educate the Consumer to Make Intelligent Choices

Within the health care industry, the most cutting edge hospitals and medical centers are realizing that their patients are, in fact, their customers, and that those customers want the same kind of choices that they are afforded in real life. "Patients being viewed as customers is a totally foreign concept in health care management," said James T. Lussier, chief executive officer of St. Charles Medical Center in Bend, Oregon. Traditionally, hospitals approach patients as if they have no other choices. Lussier asks, "Would you go into Nordstrom if the first thing they did was stick you in a waiting room and say 'I'll be back in an hour'?"

When he was promoted from president to CEO at St. Charles in 1989, Lussier envisioned a hospital that combined the operating efficiencies of top manufacturing companies with the customer-service emphasis of top retailers. "Our competition is not the hospital down the road or some doctor's office," said Lussier. "It is the standards that are being set by the Nordstroms, Lands' Ends, and Staples of the world. Patients want to know why those standards can be achieved at those companies, but not with us."

Choices are essential at St. Charles. "I think multiple offerings are especially critical in health care primarily because the general public tends to perceive health care as including primarily doctors and hospitals," said Lussier. The system has been rather exclusive, that is, anything that doctors don't feel comfortable with summarily gets excluded from consideration. As an example, I hear patients all the time saying things like, "I'm going to an orthopedist, but I can't tell my orthopedist that I'm also going to a chiropractor."

St. Charles has approached this situation in a wide variety of ways. The medical center is making major thrusts into preventative programs and education that empower patients to feel in control, and making sure that patients know that if there is an issue that they are interested in, then the medical center is interested in it as well.

Part of St. Charles' mission statement is to educate the patient to make intelligent choices. "Empowerment is not just about consent to procedures," explained Lussier. "It's about knowing every possible approach to a particular illness or disease and being able to make informed decisions." Coordinating the communication between a patient and his or her different doctors—who may have philosophical disagreements with each other's practice—has been difficult. Still it's important to make sure the patient knows what the different approaches might be. Of course, it's not always easy to offer this type of service. "One of the issues that we have to face is that it's very difficult for us to control the behavior of a physician outside the confines of the hospital," said Lussier. "We've got to bring those doctors into the orbit of the hospital. One way of doing that has been adding different services to the hospital, such as massage therapy and music therapy."

Lussier believes that the hospital has two prime customers. One is the physician, who exerts primary control over what patients have access to and what the hospital can do for the patient. The other is the patient and, by extension, the general public. "We've actually utilized patient education to bring about change in the physicians' approaches to practices. The patient will come into a doctor's office in a totally different frame of mind after being educated as to the various alternatives for treatment," said Lussier, who admits that, "Doctors have been known to get together to fire the renegade administrator who is pushing the envelope too far."

St. Charles regularly conducts educational forums and offers a wide variety of patient services:

> *For example, we have an institute for health and medicine that is very symptoms-related. It is not treatment, per se. It's looking at lifestyle, how people manage stress, and how we can educate them as to what the various alternatives are before they ever get into the acute health care system. The patients who participate become very knowledgeable about their particular practices and approach to diabetes or heart disease. They are not so willing to jump straight into having a bypass surgery or angioplasty. They know that they might be helped by some changes in diet or they might find a better alternative to manage stress.*

Lussier admits that St. Charles is only part way toward its goal of dramatically changing the attitude of physicians regarding offering patients a wide variety of choices so that those patients can be participants in their own healing. "The problem with the old health care system is that the physicians designed it," said Lussier. "They are very interested in designing the new system, but that's not going to happen. The consumer is going to design it."

It's not surprising that physicians generally are divided into two camps. Some are "really getting excited about the new customer-driven business model that affects us all," said Lussier. "But there are others who resist wholeheartedly." Lussier believes that the Internet is going to continue to have an increasingly profound impact on all aspects of health care, not only on hospital services but also on how physicians manage their practices. He predicts that eventually every doctor will offer patients a choice of consulting that doctor's Web site and the ability to communicate via e-mail.

With the surplus of healthcare-related Web sites popping up all over the Internet, if patients can't access the information they need from their physician, they will get it somewhere else, such as through their insurance plans. These days, patients are no longer compelled to physically visit a doctor's office to find out what their alternatives are. They have the choice of doing their own research from home and as a result are able to ask better questions as they and their doctors work through to decisions.

St. Charles uses a variety of methods to get the word out to patients that its many services are available. Although the hospital uses public service announcements and direct advertising, the primary vehicle is personal contact. "About 60,000 people from Bend and Central Oregon have some sort of contact with St. Charles either via visiting the Emergency Room or being admitted as a patient, or having experienced out-patient services," explained Lussier. "So, they see the valuable additional services that we offer and experience our desire to inform the patients about all their options first hand. It's word of mouth that is the most powerful differentiator in our business, so we depend on our customers to spread the news. People in this region are aware of the choices we offer."

Feed the Children: Make Life Easy for Your Customers

Feed the Children, may be a nonprofit charity, but this international hunger relief organization must still function as an effective business. Management understands that donors respond to choices, and the more choices they have, the more often they will donate—and perhaps in increasing amounts.

Based in Oklahoma City, Oklahoma, Feed the Children is a provider of emergency services in times of hurricane, flood, earthquake, and even manmade disasters such as the Oklahoma City bombing. The organization's priorities are providing food, education, and medical assistance. As explained by Paul Bigham, vice president of donor relations:

> *Feed the Children is a conduit through which donors can accomplish what they want to. We match up needs with resources. Our job is to match those who have the resources—and who want to give—with those who have the needs. We treat every donor like an individual. There are economic realities that we have to deal with, but our goal is to be as close to each individual as we possibly can; it makes economic sense to do so. Feed the Children operates primarily through its own valuable transportation system. For example, we may know that there are goods available in San Francisco and that there are people who need them in Los Angeles.*

The organization has more than seventy trucks that are dispatched to pick up food, diapers, mops, brooms, and shovels or whatever needs to be picked up and delivered to wherever the needs are. "We can arrange the pick up and delivery of those goods from Point A to Point B, whether with our own vehicles or some other means, such as drop shipping. We don't move anything unless it's consumable. Once something reaches its shelf life, it has X amount of days by government standards to be consumed without creating a harm to the public," Bigham told me.

The organization works with a broad network of 6,300 large partner organizations, such as the Dallas/Ft. Worth Metroplex Food Bank, which have both the capacity to store goods and the connections to downline the goods to an even broader network of some 25,000 smaller community service providers in all fifty states and the District of Columbia.

Bigham compared Feed the Children's network to a typical marketing distribution system of wholesalers and retailers—from Frito-Lay to the local IGA supermarket. For example, Feed the Children had a donor in Orange County, California, who wanted to sponsor a truckload of food. (A truckload can range from 25,000 to 45,000 pounds of food, depending on the goods in the shipment.) Feed the Children found a lead partner organization—in this case, the Orange County Rescue Mission, which has a system of a couple of dozen smaller groups, such as soup kitchens, church pantries, and local food banks, which distribute the goods into the community.

Increasingly, according to Bigham, the crucial choice for donors is finding an organization equipped to pick up and distribute the goods. Quite often, a manufacturer of a food product finds itself—for a variety of reasons—stuck with excess product that must be disposed of to make room in their warehouses for new product. Rather than throwing these goods into the dump, manufacturers want to find a way to get them to the individuals who need them. And they must be reassured that these goods won't be sold on the black market, resold to a third party, or subject to any kind of product liability. That's where Feed the Children comes in. Larry

Jones, the evangelist who founded and heads the organization, has committed to picking up anything that's
available within 72 hours. Bigham explained:

> *For example, if a diaper manufacturer finds itself
> with diapers on their warehouse floor that they need
> to get rid of right now, we can go and pick them up
> and distribute them. We try to make it easy as pos-
> sible on our customers—who, in our case are called
> donors—by giving them as many ways to give as we
> are physically and structurally set up to do. When
> we can't do that, we try to create a way so that
> donors can give what they want to give in the way
> that they want to give it. We find ways to do good
> things with product that normally can't get into the
> stream of commerce.*

Like any other freight transportation company, Feed
the Children calls on customers and receives calls from
customers. "We will call on manufacturers of beverages
or snack foods or canned goods or diapers or building
materials and tell them that we need X product for Y
people and we need it by Z date," said Bigham. "If they
can do it, they will; if they can't, they don't. That's the
basis we work on. If you've got it, that's great. If not,
we'll try you next time. They always have the choice to
help or not to help." Sometimes the call is initiated by
the donor/customer. Bigham recalled one instance
where a major beverage company discovered a typo-
graphical error on labels that it had already applied to
its bottles. After the company calculated that it was
cheaper to dispose of the bottles than it would be to remove the labels and put on new ones, they contacted
Feed the Children, but with one primary stipulation: the

product could not be distributed in the company's normal markets.

"We said we could send it internationally for them," added Bigham, who noted that Feed the Children has provided assistance to more than 75 countries. "They asked where it would go. We told them. We arranged everything for them. The company was excited because (1) we disposed of the product for them, (2) it didn't have to be poured down the drain, and (3) children in this third-world country were able to be treated to this incredible beverage that had just one flaw—a typo on the label. Those kids didn't care what the label said. It was a gift from heaven."

Another time, a donor needed to get rid of a boatload of bananas because of tariff considerations, and asked what Feed the Children could do with it. "We said, 'Give us 30 minutes and we'll figure it out,' " Bigham recalled. "We picked it up in a port in the South and were able to give it to service providers in the Carolinas and Georgia, who distributed the bananas to rescue missions, soup kitchens, and individuals in the country and the inner cities. That was a real delicacy for the people who needed it. That was a very unusual situation, but we had the capacity to move those bananas."

Feed the Children affords individual donors the choice of where they want their donation to be sent, domestic or international. They can earmark their gift to virtually any community or organization in America as long as it's economically feasible. "Some organizations can't do that because of their structure, size, longevity of existence, and so on," said Bigham. "We can't always do it internationally because of government restrictions. But we are able to get more food into restrictive countries than most any other organizations because we have a network system set up to do that."

Donors have a wide variety of options for giving. A donor could send a check for a single gift that would allow Feed the Children to purchase food at the price of 14 cents a pound. A donor could join an affinity group with other donors called the "Thousand-Pound Club," which sponsors the purchase of a thousand (or two thousand or three thousand, etc.) pounds of food. Another option is to buy a total sponsorship of the costs of a truckload of food—weighing between 25,000 and 45,000 pounds)—or a partial share, ranging from a six-teenth to a half. In 1999, the cost of that truckload was $5,400. For that sponsorship contribution, Feed the Children provides the donor with tangible, physical involvement with its service. For example, an individual who wants to sponsor a truckload of food can come to that food drop and be on site and watch it be unloaded and distributed. Bigham recalled:

We had one gentleman who grew up in Williamson County, West Virginia, which is near the depth of Appalachian poverty. He grew up a barefoot coal boy living up in the hollers [hollows]. He became very successful and today is the owner of several automobile dealerships in Central Florida. He wanted to sponsor two truckloads of food for the impoverished county where he grew up. He went back with us and watched that food being unloaded. He didn't want to say a word. He didn't want to be spotlighted or interviewed on radio, television, or newspapers. He just wanted to put food back into that county. When he was asked to speak, he couldn't. He was so choked up; he had a lump in his throat. His wife spoke for *him. Look what this gentleman bought for $5,400. That was his choice.*

Operating on founder Larry Jones' philosophy that there is no wrong way to feed a hungry child, Feed the Children's attitude on providing choices is that, "If we can legally, morally, and economically structure a gift that accomplishes what the donor wants to accomplish, then we'll do it; we'll find a way within those parameters," said Bigham. Talking about Jones, Bigham went on:

Larry is a pastor, a minister, an evangelist, and a humanitarian. He's also very entrepreneurial and an astute businessman. Ever since he founded and started this organization in 1979, he knew that unless you give good service and offer a good product, people aren't going to buy from you. In this case, if we don't have a good service, people aren't going to donate.

One of the things that we are seeing in the general marketplace is convenience in packaging. We are seeing that as well in the philanthropic and humanitarian areas. As a result, we are constantly looking for ways to package humanitarian and philanthropic efforts in the most expedient manner.

One of the true essentials of fund-raising and development is watching the numbers; watching the market. We are very market driven. We are reflective of where the market is going and what the market wants to do—if it fits within our charter. It's almost an arrogant stance if you don't move with the market. You'll dry up and blow way and your service will dry up and blow away. Why not feed more children by following where the market has an interest? We don't do massive market research, but we watch our numbers. When we send an appeal out, we watch how the response comes back in. When we talk about Country A or State A, and people don't support it, we get the message that that's not an area they want to support. The reality is that there are certain countries that don't generate a huge interest in support. If we talk about Country B or State B and people send in their gifts, we say, this is what people want to do. People can be extremely specific—they'll want food delivered, for example, only to Hazard County, Tennessee—or they might be more general: deliver it anywhere east of the Mississippi River.

But even if the market does not favor a particular country, that doesn't mean Feed the Children will not try to help that country. When donors fill out a form directing where they want their money to go, they have the option of checking a box that says, "Where Needed Most," which enables Feed the Children to make the decision where disposable, discretionary funds can be spent. Bigham said the organization does not want to be so market driven that they end up sacrificing who they are.

Feed the Children offers a variety of options for individuals and corporations to participate in their programs. Individuals can designate a donation to be deducted from their paycheck or their checking or savings accounts. They can give a straight cash gift or donate a product or both. Companies can help sponsor events or concerts. They can arrange for their employees to unload food or other products from Feed the Children trucks as a community project.

Many corporations find that a tie-in with Feed the Children translates into goodwill in the community and improved sales. For example, the owner of an oil-changing service once advertised that for three weeks, he would earmark $5.00 out of every $19.95 oil change in his 27 different locations for Feed the Children. "He received great exposure on television, radio, and newspapers," said Bigham. "He got people feeling good about him. He expanded his public profile. He created better brand-awareness and loyalty. This was part of his personal and spiritual and humanitarian beliefs."

Feed the Children is associated with several high-visibility entertainers and sports people, such as recording stars Garth Brooks, B.B. King, and Ricky Skaggs and Dallas Cowboy football stars Troy Aikman and Emmitt Smith. "Garth Brooks has a real heart for hungry children," Bigham told me. "He's looking for a way to help get food out to those who need it. When he has a concert, he asks people to bring a can of food and give it to Feed the Children. That's a choice for him."

Charitable organizations are all keenly aware that over the next several years, trillions of dollars in wealth will be transferred as the older generation passes on. The people planning their estates are faced with a myriad of choices of where that money should best go—to the government, to their children, or to a nonprofit.

As a nonprofit, Feed the Children offers people the choice of shielding or deferring taxes. Feed the Children can be designated in an estate as a trust or a charitable remainder trust; it can receive a bequest. If a donor doesn't want to give cash, he has the option of donating through stock transfers or appreciated assets. A donor could also set up a perpetuating charitable legacy or get his or her name on a wall or a building or a project. It all comes back to choices.

"In 24 years of working in nonprofits, I've found that, above all, donors want to have confidence in a system," said Bigham. "Donors have donor remorse just like buyers have buyer remorse. They ask themselves: Did I make the right decision? Is this organization going to do what they said they were going to do? It's up to us to reinforce to that donor that (1) they've made a good choice, because it is going where they want it to go; and that (2) we have used that dollar economically and efficiently, so they see they have made a wise decision.

"So, we send back information to the donors—not substantiating every single dollar that comes through—but substantiating the programs that we have, giving a tangible, visible, aural representation of where that dollar went and how it was used. People don't want to give the guy or lady on the street a dollar. They want to give the dollar to the organization that has the structure so they can see that the dollar goes for food."

All businesses can benefit from attempting to predict questions from their customers. The people at Feed the Children understand that they also have to answer the question that the donor is thinking to himself, but does not say out loud: What's in it for me?

"When a donor asks that question," says Bigham, "we have a long list of answers. We can say, 'Your donation went where you wanted it to go, it was economically delivered, it reached people that you couldn't reach by yourself, it protected you from being in the environs where you don't want to be in. The essence of truth in all we do is to try to answer that question so that the customer is satisfied." On a spiritual level, sometimes people give because they want to have certain spiritual precepts reinforced. "At Feed the Children," said Bigham, "we are doing what we do from both a professional perspective and a spiritual perspective because we know that 'there but for the grace of God go I.'"

Mike's Express Carwash: Help the Customer to Make Sound Decisions

Some companies are popular because they've simplified the buying process by making all the choices for you. One of those companies is Mike's Express Carwash, a 19-unit chain of automated carwashes based in Indianpolis, Indiana, which offers its customers speed, high quality, and attentive service.

Mike's offers customers a variety of choices. There's a package that includes a wash, Mike's Clear Coat (a specially formulated product that adds shine and protection to a car) and Wheel Bright (a process that removes the brake dust to product shiny and clean wheels), as well as another package that includes a wash, Mike's Clear Coat and an underbody wash. The deluxe package is called "The Works," which comprises a wash, and underbody wash, Mike's Clear Coat, and Wheel Bright. Machines perform all of these tasks, which are also available a la carte.

"The concept is that the customer stays in the car, and when he leaves, it's completely cleaned, dry, and shiny," explained Bill Dahm, whose father and uncle started the family company in 1948, and ran it for 30 years as a full-service business. "I emphasize the word 'dry.' In many exterior carwashes, the customer has to get out with a towel and dry their own car. We have all the technology that provides for detail-oriented quality in a very short period of time."

As Dahm sees it, the typical carwash has what he called "task interference." The operators of that kind of carwash "come up with all these things that customers want. But they don't realize that trying to be everything to all people, slows your operation down. "If an operation like ours runs too slow, people will choose not to come often because we live in a society where people's time is the currency."

Mike's Carwash does not offer customers the choice of having the inside of the car cleaned because that job is too labor-intensive and time-consuming. Instead, it does provide high-suction vacuum cleaners to customers who want to clean the interior themselves. Mike also provides space on its property for people to do that. A vending machine supplies extra cleaning supplies for windows and dashboards. Again, all of those materials are for self-service. Offering lower grade service of non-specialty tasks is a good tactic for all businesses that have to factor in the customer's time. Explains Dahm:

For a dollar, you get four minutes of sweep time. Many customers don't do that every time. They may wash it three times, and on the fourth time, do the sweeping. Mike's is selling actual speed as well as the perception of speed to its customers. At most car-washes, you drive by and you'll see 20 or 30 people waiting. At ours, it's three or four. People driving by see that they can get right in and right out. There is a psychological factor; long lines influence a person's decision of whether it's worth taking the time to get their carwash.

"Most people don't go to carwashes to just visit," Dahm quipped. "It takes too long. I've never seen any carwash company that gets its customer in and out faster than we do. They are in and out in two minutes. Very seldom will you see a line at our carwash. That's why we call our concept Mike's Express. We started using the word Express before it was popular, back in 1978. Some companies give people all kinds of choices, but a simple approach to choices work for us. One of the biggest things we're selling is a very fast experience."

Continental Airlines: Offer Customers Choices They Will Pay For

Gordon Bethune, the chairman and chief executive officer of Continental Airlines, takes a refreshingly realistic view toward providing his airline's passengers with choices:

> *Just asking people what they want, they'll write you an epistle. So, we don't ask customers what they want. We ask them what they want that they will pay for. If they won't pay for it, we don't feel the need to work on it because it adds no value. Passengers would like extra legroom, but they won't pay for it. Passengers want somebody who is nice, who does what they say they're going to do, and who gets them to their destination on time.*

Like every other airline, Continental offers the usual choices—First Class or Coach seating; aisle or window; chicken or fish—but it also offers choices of how customers want to buy their seats. "You've got different kinds of customers, so you have to use the mode that they want to buy from you," Bethune told me:

> *Some people are 100-percent price sensitive. They don't care about Continental or any other airline. We need to know that. So, we and other airlines sell our excess, distressed inventory on Web sites such as Priceline.com, where the customer doesn't know which airline he is going to take or how many stops he's going to make. That customer just cares about*

the price. If that's what he wants, we've got it for him.

The second category of customer is loyal to Continental and wants the best fare while taking advantage of the company's frequent flyer program or service levels. Those people come to the Continental Web site, which offers lowest price Continental airfares. "We guarantee that you will not find a cheaper Continental ticket than what you can buy on our Web site. You might find a match, but you won't find it for less," Bethune promises.

The customer in the third category wants to view Continental in the context of United, Delta, American, and others. So in mid-2000, Continental and 26 other carriers banded together for ownership of a Web site that is managed by a third party and will have a hyperlink to each airline's Web site. Unlike online travel Web sites, where airlines pay for preferential placement, the new site, called Hotwire.com, will offer a customer an objective look at prices, according to Hotwire.

My favorite Continental Airlines' choice is the option to carry on a bag that is bigger than those allowed by the other major carriers. Bethune was moved to make that decision when he was flying out of the San Diego airport and witnessed a confrontation between security guards and a Continental passenger over the size of a bag that was too large, according to the baggage "sizer" that was installed by Delta Airlines, which manages the security contract for the concourse Continental uses at that airport. Continental ticket agents ultimately escorted the passenger through security by explaining that the bag conformed to Continental's specifications. If you fly a lot and prefer to carry on your luggage, that's a choice you can appreciate. In that and many other ways, the airline ensures that the customer has a set of unique options if they chose to fly Continental. This type of strategy is applicable to any business.

KEY WAYS TO OFFER CHOICE

The best customer-service companies provide their clients with a plethora of options because the more options the more likely the customer will prefer to do business with you rather than with your competition. The following key questions and strategies will help you to evaluate how your business addresses the issue of offering choice:

- Are you providing your customers with choices, or are you a one-size-fits-all business?
- Examine the choices you offer your customers.
- Evaluate whether those choices are adequate.
- Examine the choices your competition offers your customers and respond to that difference.
- Use choices as a tool to greater sales and greater customer relationships.
- Make sure all your employees are aware of—and can talk about—all of your choices.
- Provide your customer with alternatives—rather than having to say "No."
- Provide your customers with several different—and effective—ways to contact you.
- Educate your customer to make sound choices.
- Figure out which choices the customer is willing to pay for.

 # Create an Inviting Place

Be not forgetful to entertain strangers,
for thereby some have entertained
angels unawares.

—Hebrews 13:2

The interior of the storefront—the feeling, layout, design, lighting, seating, wide aisles, larger fitting rooms, display fixtures, amenities, and, of course, the merchandise—is yet another facet of customer service the Nordstrom way. With convenience and openness as the trademarks of its store design, Nordstrom wants to make it as easy as possible for customers to circulate and shop throughout the entire store, and for sales associates to be visible to help customers do just that. The store is comfortable with many cushy chairs and sofas to sit down in. A piano played by a live person is Nordstrom's signature service for engaging a customer's senses. If shoppers need any kind of special assistance, a concierge is at the ready with helpful information about the store or to call a cab for you or to recommend a restaurant. Need to send a fax? They'll do that for you. Need to check your coat, umbrella, and packages with the concierge? No problem.

The Customer Service department in each store offers check-cashing privileges for Nordstrom cardholders, immediate posting of payments to Nordstrom accounts, answers to inquiries regarding those accounts, monthly statements, credit line increases, complimentary gift wrapping, and purchase of gift certificates.

In addition to four different kinds of restaurants, a number of stores also have salons that provide facials, massage, and other beauty treatments. Some of the larger stores have a SPA Nordstrom, which offers natural aromatherapy, herbal body wrap, massage therapy, natural sport manicures, and aromatic facials. Inexpensive shoeshines are available in the men's area as well.

Having created the kind of pleasant, inviting place where most women feel extremely comfortable, Nordstrom became the logical retailer to pioneer in-store mammograms. In 1998, two members of the oncology steering committee of the Evanston and Glenbrook Hospitals in suburban Chicago asked Michele Love, manager at the Nordstrom store at the Old Orchard Shopping Center in Skokie to install the mammography center, which, they thought, would seem less threatening in a department store. (Nordstrom had already donated money to open two breast-health libraries at the hospitals.) Love agreed to donate space to the hospitals, who oversaw the renovation of the Health and Beauty Center at the Skokie store—renamed the Breast Health and Mammography Center—and provided it with a state-of-the-art, low-dose mammography machine and film processor. The two hospitals also staffed and marketed the program, which Nordstrom helped promote. The mammograms are read by radiologists at the hospitals and faxed to the referring physicians' offices. With the overwhelming positive reception to the mammography center, Nordstrom has added centers in several of its other stores, and other department stores have followed suit. Nordstrom's commitment to treating customers as people is genuine and widespread. The commitment to breast cancer awareness was a natural result of creating an inviting place.

Although every year, 182,000 women are diagnosed with breast cancer, and 46,000 die from the disease, many women don't get mammograms. Projects such as the Breast Health and Mammography Center are helping to change that. A Nordstrom customer in suburban Denver told the Gannett News Service that she decided to go to the Nordstrom store at the Park Meadows Mall, because it was a familiar and comfortable environment, which made the examination "a pleasant experience. . . . They gave me a pager so that I could shop," instead of having to sit in the waiting room, and "they had nice terry-cloth robes (for the patients) to put on in the (waiting) area. Talk about customer service."

As you're reading this, you're probably thinking: My business isn't set up to offer a concierge service, herbal body wraps, and mammograms or shoe shines. Relax. It does not have to be. But can your business accommodate clean restrooms and careful provision of necessary services?

A couple of years ago, two female reporters from the *Washington Post* surveyed the ladies restrooms in all the department stores in the Washington, D.C. area. Their criteria were all the things we look for in a good restroom—ample space and supplies, cleanliness, diaper-changing facilities, and so on. Nordstrom was rated Number One. We don't usually associate clean restrooms with customer service, but why not? When your restrooms are clean and well supplied, you are telling your customer that you care about every aspect of their experience with your company.

Shoji Tabuchi, a Japanese born-and-raised singer-fiddler, has became one of the most popular acts in Branson, Missouri, by creating an inviting place for his loyal fans, who flock to his 2,000-seat theater. He has drawn so many patrons to the southwestern Missouri town (which bills itself as the Live-Entertainment Capital of the World) that the state gave him a special award for his contributions to Missouri tourism.

The president of the Branson Chamber of Commerce credited Mr. Tabuchi's popularity on customer service and word-of-mouth advertising. Mr. Tabuchi takes nothing for granted. During the intermissions of his shows, he mingles with the audience. Most people travel to Branson by bus, and then at the end of the show, he boards each bus to say goodbye. Audience members fill out comment cards, which are entered into a computerized database used for mailings. When those people return, Mr. Tabuchi will have a record of their birthdays and anniversaries, which he will announce with much to-do during the show.

Mr. Tabuchi's show has been described as a "wholesome spectacle," with a cast of 80 and a potpourri of music and dance from bluegrass to polka, Hawaiian to gospel, with motorcycles, Western ropers, and hula dancers, accompanied by a $2 million laser system. The theater's bathrooms are lavish, with lavender-crystal chandeliers. The basins in the ladies' room are festooned with fresh orchids; the men's room is decorated in an Edwardian motif, complete with a billiard table and fireplace. The theater, which puts on between eight and twelve shows a week for people in wheelchairs, provides special escorts who assist frail or disabled passengers to get on and off their buses and to and from restrooms. A staff member said that such indulging is intended to send a simple message to customers: "This show is different. You are important."

Is your place of business an "inviting place"? Do you make customers feel that they are important? It's easy to find the answers to those questions. The next time you go to work, pretend you've never been there before. Pretend you are the customer. What do you see? What don't you see? What do you like? Would you like spending time there if you didn't have to? You'll know soon enough if customers feel welcome.

But what if your business isn't a "place" at all. Perhaps it's a Web site. It doesn't matter if your storefront is real or virtual; the same principles apply. Is your Web site easy to access? Does it take forever to download? Is your typeface easy to run? Is the site easy to navigate? When you get there, is the site dynamic and exciting? The great customer-service-oriented Web sites such as Amazon.com understand that they are not just selling things; they are involved in transactions, which will lead to other transactions. That's why their sites are inviting in every sense of the word.

Realty Executives of Nevada: Greet Your Customers with a Smile

When a prospective home buyer or seller walks into the Las Vegas office of Realty Executives of Nevada—one of the hottest real estate companies in one of the hottest real estate markets in the country—the first thing they see is the smiling face of receptionist Crystal Zuke. "Since I am the first person they meet, I am the first thing they relate with Realty Executives," said Crystal.

"The most important thing is to make sure you connect with that person. So, it's very important to me to be always positive and smiling. Because nobody is going to be offended by a smile."

Anyone who has ever bought and/or sold a home knows what a nerve-wracking, anxiety-provoking experience it can be. Sometimes Crystal becomes the innocent target of their distress and frustration. She knows that that comes with the territory. She said:

> There are people who come in screaming; they are so nervous. This is a big step for them; some transactions involve millions of dollars. Their whole livelihood is riding on these papers and they want to make sure that they are being taken care of. I just keep smiling and am as helpful and patient with them as I can be. If there is someone on the phone who has got something that's falling apart, and he or she needs that agent right away, I just take it on myself to make sure that they get that agent right away. Eventually, they calm down and you can rationalize with them.

Having recently bought a house for the first time with her husband, Crystal tells clients that she has been in their place and can relate to what they are going through. "I tell them that it gets better," she said. "You'll move and you'll be happy." Most importantly, if a client gets upset, "I don't take it personally, because it's nothing I've done. You have to shake it off because if you let that build up inside of you, you'd go crazy. My husband wouldn't want to live with me anymore," she said with a laugh.

Once she takes her post at 8:30 in the morning, Crystal makes sure she gets up as little as possible. "If you walked into a building, you would not want to see an empty desk," Crystal told me. "You want to see a smiling face who can help you. Not somebody on the phone, not somebody on the computer."

When clients come into the office—one of four offices that Realty Executives occupies in the Las Vegas area—Crystal asks them to have a seat and offers them something to drink. "I want to give them the quickest most efficient service that I can provide," she explained. "I get the agent for them right away. If they are picking up something, I get that for them right away. The customer always takes precedence. My ability to serve them is what they are going to associate with Realty Executives from now on. So, I have to make sure I leave a good impression in their minds."

As the receptionist in an extremely busy real estate agency, Crystal has to serve two sets of constituents—not only the clients, but the independent agents themselves (she keeps their files organized)—and keep them both happy.

In addition to dealing with the controlled chaos in the office, Crystal also covers the telephone during lunches and breaks. As the public voice for the company, she has to have a smile in her voice as well as on her face. "The person who is calling in cannot see what I'm doing," she explained. "So being attentive to them is very important. They can't see that there are 60 people standing at my desk. All they know is that they are on the other end and they want some service—as soon as possible."

I once asked Bruce Nordstrom, the co-chairman emeritus of Nordstrom, who trains his salespeople. His answer was: "their parents." Crystal Zukc says the same is true for her:

> *My parents always taught me to be positive. The first impression you make is going to stick with people over the long run, so you should make sure it's a positive first impression. If you can't focus on the positive, then there is something lacking and you need to find what's lacking and accommodate for it. We work very hard to make sure we have an upbeat, positive environment. No matter how bad things are looking, no matter how far behind you are, you still have to focus on the positive—even if the only positive thing you can think about is that at 5:30 you get to go home.*

Does your business have a Crystal Zuke to make your clients feel that they are being taken care of? If not, why not? Although Crystal's job does not directly involve selling, she is a profit center for Realty Executives, just in the way she treats customers.

Continental Airlines: Make the Customer Feel Comfortable

When Gordon Bethune became chairman and CEO of Continental Airlines, the carrier was an amalgamation of several merged mediocre airlines. "We had four or five different exterior paint schemes, and because of cost-cutting, the only thing the paint jobs had in common was that they were all peeling," Bethune recalled. "The seat covers were mismatched; the carpeting was usually soiled. All of that was unprofessional. It reflected the way that our employees felt about our product. They work on those airplanes; it's their living office."

Right off the bat, Bethune mandated that Continental was going to clean the airplanes on a more frequent basis and make sure that they had a uniform interior and exterior look. "Today, we are meticulous in the way we clean the interior and keep the appearance up, and we have a 100-percent common paint scheme, which is very dependable and reliable. It's like coming home," declared Bethune. "When we started cleaning the airplanes every day, the biggest benefactors were our employees. That's their professional pride."

Bethune characterizes the cleaning of Continental's 380 airplanes as, "the cheese on the pizza. It costs money to put cheese on a pizza. But that's why people buy the pizza. They say, 'I like Gordon's pizza because it has lots of cheese.' More important, once you become dependable and reliable, it's cheaper over the long run. You don't have extraordinary things happening. You don't have overtime. You don't have disruptive operations. We've learned that it's better to pay up front."

Continental inspects its interiors every three days, including the smallest details like checking the reading lightbulbs, which Bethune describes as "a big issue with customers." Every airplane that goes through Continental's Houston hub gets a tailwash whether it needs it or not.

As we mentioned in Chapter 1, at a time when other carriers are restricting the size of carry-on baggage, Continental has taken a stand in favor of both passengers and crew. Every one of Continental's aircraft has closets for coats and baggage, as well as the biggest overhead bins that can be safely installed. Those bins are equipped on every Continental plane because the airline wants to make sure the passenger has a consistent experience. That expansion of storage space cost Continental some $20 million.

If you fly as much as I do—and if you prefer to carry on your luggage, as I do—you will salute Continental Airlines for taking this stand. "There are very rigid standards at other airlines," said Bethune:

They have a one-size-fits-all mentality at their security checkpoints. So, even if you are a Platinum Elite, first-class ticket holder, you get the lowest common denominator on the baggage size. Do the math: There are four seats across in first class and six seats across in coach. So, in first class, you're paying for a seat and a half. So, why wouldn't you get the extra bag? We offer you that. We understand that you shouldn't worry that the materials you need for your presentation—or your change of underwear—might get lost if you had to check your baggage. We want to make sure you can have them both. We do that even though most of our competitors refuse to do that.

In early 2000, Delta Air Lines ended up agreeing with Continental's position. Delta, the world's largest carrier announced that it was going to retrofit the overhead bins in most of its airplanes to provide more storage space for carry-ons. After going through a three-month trial period with some of its aircraft, Delta found that the more spacious bins helped in boarding the airplane five to eight minutes faster because passengers didn't have to struggle to find storage and could be seated more quickly.

Bethune, a former executive at The Boeing Company convinced officials at the Seattle aircraft maker to back him on this stand. "That's why we bought bigger airplanes like the 777 with overhead bins that are bigger than the DC10s. That's what passengers want and we can safely store the bags. Why would we treat people on a 777 as if they were flying on a DC10? We don't have a winner and a loser with a baggage issue. We are not going to be at odds with our customer. We've attracted a huge ridership and the loyalty of people who want this consistent level in the way they are treated, taken to their destination on time, and the way their bags are delivered. Customers want and will pay for extra baggage space. We are going to provide that. Our employees understand that."

Restrooms are another key issue in creating an inviting aircraft on which to fly. Responding to complaints by passengers and crew, Continental spent $36 million to install mid-cabin bathrooms in most of its 737 jet planes, which were originally used for short-haul flights, but are now being used for longer flights. The company has also bought aircraft equipped with bigger, specially designed restrooms for passengers with physical disabilities. For its regional subsidiary airline, Continental Express, Continental selected a 50-seat aircraft that has a restroom bigger than those on a DC10. "That was one of the reasons that we picked that airplane," said Bethune.

When it comes to seats, Continental has found that most customers are more interested in cheaper fares than seating comfort. Although everyone wants a seat that reclines a bit, up to 10 percent of the economy seats in a commercial aircraft do not recline because of space constraints. Continental can't change that reality, but it does provide its reservation agents with the information on the seats that don't recline, so they can pass it on to the customers.

While some airlines have talked about eliminating some seats in their aircraft to create more space, Bethune called that approach a "fad" to get rid of excess capacity. "You have to think about your employees' morale," he said. "Those seats you're removing are employees' seats. And if you don't have good employee morale in the airline business, you don't have anything."

Callison Architecture: Create Multidimensional Space

When it comes to the Nordstrom idea of creating an inviting place, the experts work at Callison Architecture, the Seattle-based firm that has designed the last 75 Nordstrom stores out of the 97 in the chain. In addition, the last two directors of store planning at Nordstrom are former partners with Callison. No wonder Callison considers itself the Nordstrom of the architecture business. The firm provides architecture, planning, interiors, and graphic design for urban mixed-use developments, retail and entertainment facilities, corporate office environments, hospitality and residential buildings, and health care facilities. Callison projects include Deira City Centre, a retailing center in Dubai, United Arab Emirates; and The Grand Gateway, a 3.3 million square foot mixed-use development in Shanghai, China, as well as two facilities featured in this book: W Seattle Hotel and St. Charles Medical Center in Bend, Oregon.

The reception area at the Callison offices in the heart of downtown Seattle reflects the philosophy of an inviting place. Located near a staircase on the second floor of the four floors the firm occupies, the reception area is designed to be a beehive of activity. Everyone who works at the firm has to go through that lobby space to get anything done. Partner Stan Laegreid told me:

*It sends two very positive messages: (1) Clients in-
stantly feel that they are a part of everything that's
happening and (2) our people are a resource. We're
saying that our most important thing isn't necessarily the models of our projects on display. It's the people who are walking back and forth, and you're going
to see them in the lobby. It's an engaging, tactile environment. It's a friendly space for our clients and
our employees. Approachable. Comfortable. Casual.*

M.J. Munsell, another Callison partner, believes
that a trademark of the firm is creating spaces that are
multidimensional, and very sociable and comfortable for
the end user. "It's essential to continue to learn about—
and capitalize on—how people live and work and play,"
she said. "Those three functions of our lives are merg-
ing, and all of our projects take that into account:
health care becomes shopping because we all have so
little time. With office space, we need to get more done
than just work in the office. Retail spaces are for more
than shopping. That thinking starts to pervade most of
the products we work on."

A good example of that thinking is the downtown
Seattle U.S. Bank Centre building, which Callison designed in the early 1990s. The lobby of the 48-story office building includes three Starbucks Coffee locations
(this is Seattle, after all), a bank branch, high-end retail, including Barneys New York and the FAO Schwarz
toy store. The second floor has additional retail as well
as two movie theaters; and the third floor features the
dramatic Palomino restaurant. Since its creation 12
years ago, U.S. Bank Centre, which also has several
comfortable couches, has been one of the most popular
enclosed public spaces in the city.

The idea of creating an inviting place is to "give users an experience they don't get to have on their own," according to Robert Tindall, president of Callison. "So, a Nordstrom store is a very pleasant environment: plush carpets, music, displays. A lot of those customers don't have that in their own homes, so it's exciting to experience that. We spend a lot of time breaking spaces down and trying to give them a human element. The idea is not to create large and austere spaces that make you feel uncomfortable, that make you feel that you don't belong. Our approach is to make you feel comfortable, to make you feel better than how you usually feel. Retail needs clarity; because one of the things that makes you comfortable in a space is understanding where you should go and what to expect next. At the same time, we are in an era where people want more drama, more theater. You want to have clarity, but you also want to give them pleasant surprises."

Callison integrates its architecture with its image design, rather than separating them into different functions. The firm brings together branding specialists, visual merchandisers, industrial and graphic designers, and writers to help clients tell their story, and to produce different and unusual environments. "We have been helped by our relationship with Nordstrom because we've been a little bit ahead of the trend of our industry," Laegreid believed. "Nordstrom is recognized as creating more of an environment well before that became part of the consciousness of the commercial design sector. When we design Nordstrom stores, we make a very deliberate effort to make it more residential. To make people feel at home."

Laegreid recalled some sage words from John Nordstrom, co-chairman emeritus of the company, who was keenly involved with store design. At one time, some people had commented on the noise generated by a steel drum band that for many years played outside the door at the old downtown Seattle Nordstrom flagship store.

"John Nordstrom specifically said, 'You have to hear the music of the street,'" Laegreid recalled. "It's the idea of having a sensory experience, of being very much engaged to the surroundings. That's being a part of the community. That's what we're all about."

St. Charles Medical Center: Focus on a Human Element

Common sense in customer service has been essential to the strategy at St. Charles Medical Center in Bend, Oregon. "We've started with the things that are not so directly related to health care, but are real image-breakers," said chief executive officer Jim Lussier. Taking a page out of Swedish Hospital's game plan, St. Charles brought in consultants from the Ritz-Carlton hotel chain to help to improve its food service. St. Charles' highly trained staff chefs prepare excellent cuisine from a selected menu, which can be brought to the rooms for all patients and visitors 24 hours a day. The kitchen responds to an order within 10 minutes.

"That kind of feature is a symbol to patients and the community that St. Charles has changed the way it serves the patient," Lussier told me. "Once the community saw what we'd done, they began to look for other ways that the organization had changed."

For example, St. Charles provides nurses with cell phones instead of pagers, so that they can respond to calls faster and patients are not bothered by a crackling intercom. Mini-pharmacies on various hospital floors provide ready access to medicine and information.

These types of changes have as profound an influence on the staff as they do on the patient community. "When we started doing some of our fundamental changes a few years ago, they were a real awakening for our staff," recalled Lussier. In one year, management time dropped 22 percent, creating annual savings of $683,000.

To become a place where patients would be comfortable, St. Charles had to make profound changes from the bottom up. "We've changed on two major levels," Lussier explained. "The first is obviously the physical environment: We have spent a lot of money changing the physical environment of the hospital to reflect a welcoming place. Like at Nordstrom, it's all in the details, all the way down to having fresh flowers on the tables in the cafeteria and at every entrance to the hospital." The biggest compliment anybody could give St. Charles "is that we do not look like a hospital. We've done our level best to not do that."

The second major change at St. Charles was in taking care of the human element. "We used to take it for granted that most patients wanted to be here," said Lussier. "Well, guess what? We found out that they didn't want to be here. In fact, when they really got honest in surveys, they would tell us that the hospital is a really frightening place to be. Not only does their disease or illness take away a lot of their freedom, but also as soon as they get to the hospital, we take away the rest of their freedom and dignity. We shave their heads, we give them a number, we put a wristband on them, we take away all of their clothes, and give them a gown that's split down the back, and we say, 'Okay, we want you to be comfortable in this environment.' "

Today, if their condition allows it, patients can bring their own clothes from home and wear them for as long as they want in the presurgery orientation. They don't have to put on their hospital gown until they begin to get ready to go into surgery. Wearing their own clothes makes patients "a whole lot more comfortable, while they are sitting in some sterile waiting area on a stretcher in front of God and everybody," said Lussier. "It completely transforms their mental orientation. Consequently, they are much more relaxed; they have less anxiety about the procedure. They require less anesthesia. They recover quicker and they have fewer complications. These things are not just for convenience. They actually predetermine the psychological environment of the patient, and subsequently the clinical environment as well."

To make the experience a little easier for both patients and family members, and to solve a thorny parking problem, St. Charles established valet parking, which is staffed by volunteers. Again, it's the details, the small touches that add up to a positive experience.

In virtually every major expansion and redesign project, St. Charles takes into consideration how the medical center can be more efficient and customer friendly. For example, after patients complained of being cold in the old surgery center, when the new surgery center was built, one of the features added was a fireplace in the lobby. Besides obviously adding warmth, the fireplace "also completely changes the ambiance that is perceived by those patients coming in," Lussier explained. "They fully expect to see something white, something sterile, something very unfriendly. We're trying to turn that perception upside down."

St. Charles is completely carpeted. Said Lussier:

Carpet transforms the hospital. Our patients love it. It adds warmth. It improves the acoustics. It's a great way of cutting down noise, which is the number one complaint of patients and families in a hospital. All the experts said it's impossible to have carpet in a hospital because of the sterility factor. They say you can't keep carpet clean, we've done it. We've never had a sterility problem.

What would a discussion of hospital comfort be without mentioning the beds? St. Charles has been adding the latest models of hospital beds loaded with features for patient convenience, such as telephones built into the handles, and instruments for operating the bed, the television, and drapes. "All of those things have a clinical impact as well because each one of those little items is giving back to the patient some sense of control over their environment that they have lost because of their illness or disease," said Lussier.

As health care becomes an increasingly customer-sensitive business, many medical centers are taking a retail approach to their design, combining the best of both worlds into what is referred to in the health care business as "integrated medical campuses." Because people involved in the health care system are crunched for time, these integrated medical campuses become small cities, with many of the services one would need in a daily routine, including banks, pharmacies, beauty shops, bookstores, and restaurants.

Some medical centers offer valet parking, hot blankets, and a kitchen stocked with free refreshments for family members. In the highly competitive Seattle market, Swedish Medical Center has differentiated itself from its rivals with its spectacular food. Yes. Great dining in a hospital is possible. Operating under a program called À La Carte Dining, Swedish offers patients a menu of nearly 300 items, from the standard fare of fresh fruit and cottage cheese to spinach and ricotta calzone and salsa Caesar salad, with Dove Bar for dessert. Items are based upon popularity, variety, nutrition, and speed of preparation. Patients need only dial on their bedside telephone to reach the kitchen where a clerk takes the order and enters it into a computer. If the patient's doctor has prescribed a special diet or forbidden certain foods, that information will appear on the computer, and the kitchen will haggle with the patient over substitutions. The cooks will even prepare special orders if the ingredients are available in the kitchen. Because the meals are already included in their daily hospital fees, patients are allowed to order as much as they want to eat. Visiting family members and guests can order from a similar menu and pay with cash on delivery. In short, every business needs to think beyond the customer, to what or who has an impact on the customer.

Good service means breaking down what customers expect as well. Swedish Medical Center doesn't just serve good food; it offers a complete service experience. Servers, dressed in black pants, white shirt, and a tie, speedily deliver the food (usually within 30 minutes), which is served on china. "We are putting the patient in the driver's seat," offered Kris Schroeder, director of nutrition services. "Before, when meals were served with

few options, we had a lot of wasted food, untouched because it didn't appeal to some patients or they weren't
hungry at the time it was served. And that meant they
were not getting needed nutrition."

A friend of mine who had her baby at Swedish Medical Center told me that the food was so good, she didn't
want to go home. Now *that's* great food service! She's
also planning to have her next baby at Swedish proving
that supplementary services can equal return customers. Another pioneering medical center is the LDS
Hospital in Salt Lake City, Utah. A couple of years ago,
the hospital got rid of a policy stipulating that, to guard
against infection, a surgical patient had to strip down to
his underwear—regardless of the severity of the operation. This policy was a remnant from an era when patients had no choice but to totally relinquish control
upon arrival at the hospital. If you're lying on your back
on a stretcher, half-naked, you don't feel empowered by
the experience. An infection-control committee dumped
the no-underwear policy.

I particularly like one design change that was made
at the LDS Hospital. The way the hospital was set up,
pre-operation procedures were conducted at one end of
the hospital, while the actual surgery was performed
at the opposite end. Because of this arrangement, patients were forced to wait for as long as 40 minutes for
the next available wheelchair or gurney to transport
them to the operating room. Someone came up with the
bright idea that healthy patients should be allowed to
walk. You probably didn't think 90 percent of good customer service is common sense, but it is. A leader in
any business must operate on simple principles of common sense.

W Seattle: Make People Feel at Home

W Hotel's luxurious W Signature Bed doesn't come with a built-in telephone, but it is one of the reasons why, at the end of the day, the W is such an inviting place. As someone who has spent plenty of nights in a wide variety of hotel beds, I was struck by the incredible heavenly comfort of the W's bed. The bed includes a mattress pillow top that is custom-made by Simmons for the W's parent company, Starwood Hotels; it is a thick, homey, down-filled feather pillow on top of the mattress and smooth, 250-count sheets. The best hotel bed I've ever experienced; it's the kind you would want in your own home.

All of the W Hotel's down products come from Pacific Coast Feather, a local Seattle company that is one of the country's leading producers of 100 percent non-allergenic down products. W Seattle has a large number of nonallergenic pillows available upon request to satisfy wary or sensitive customers. "We'll make up the bed any way the customer wants," Limberg stated categorically. "We have the mission and the tools to do that." The lesson is: Be prepared for the worse case scenario and offer an alternative.

With so many parents traveling with small babies, W has been using special baby cribs as a differentiator between it and the competition. "What's the most near and dear thing to people? Their children. Having traveled with children myself, I saw that you could niche yourself apart from your competitors if you just handled this component properly," said Limberg. "Most of the baby cribs in hotels are beat up. They've been folded up so many times they're no longer a rectangle; they're a parallelogram. You don't know if they meet the latest safety standards for bar width. We bought the nicest chrome baby cribs we could find. And if you don't like one of those, we have the padded travel type that is built low to the floor. We got Pacific Coast Feather to supply us with a down comforter for the baby crib, so we don't have to fold up a king-size blanket."

You can always take the concept of creating an inviting place to the next level: If children are the most near and dear thing to parents, pets carry that distinction with their owners. W is one of only about 15 percent of the hotels in the country that allow a guest to keep a pet in the room. "We're pet friendly," said Limberg. "We have a pet bed that is feather-filled as well. Our motto is that 'Everybody sleeps on a W Signature Bed at W Seattle, whether you're on two legs or four.'"

The rest of the room is an entertainment center, with features such as a Sony CD player, a large-screen Mitsubishi that lets a guest surf the Internet from bed. If a guest prefers shutting out all the electronic stimuli, a miniature water fountain provides some much-appreciated Zen-like serenity.

The first physical indication that you have just entered an inviting place will be dictated by the architecture and the design. Entering the W Seattle from its Seneca Street entrance, the guest instantly sees he has alternatives. To his right, down a few stairs is an open, often crowded lounge area where people can have something to drink while mingling with—or waiting for—friends. To the left is the registration area, where a guest is accompanied by a black-clad "cast member." Just beyond the registration counter is the bank of elevators leading up to the rooms. (It's tough enough getting your bearings in a new hotel without having to search for the elevators.) Just beyond the elevators is the restaurant, which has its own entrance from Fourth Avenue. Limberg confided:

> *It's no secret that some hotels put up a wall between the restaurant and the hotel to leave no doubt about the separation between the two. We chose not to go that route. We want the flow. This whole building is designed [by Callison Architecture] to be comfortable and to flow aesthetically from a traffic standpoint. It's supposed to be easy for you to stay here.*
>
> *Many hotels are designed, built, and furnished to make life easier for the hotel and staff than for the guests. When that happens, the idea of that "inviting place" takes a backseat to practicality and durability and ease of care. There is paranoia in our industry that if you put something nice out in the lobby or other parts of the hotel that people are going to take it. The reality is that that's rarely the case. If you have a hundred artifacts in the lobby and three are missing, but you've put 10,000 people through the building, I'm not sure you have a problem. As a matter of fact, I'm sure that you don't.*

The final ingredient to make the W an inviting place is the employee. When the guest comes through the door, "We want our cast members to be welcoming and engaging. We want to create an interaction," said Limberg. "That's an opportunity for us to differentiate ourselves from our peers, and also to differentiate ourselves from the experiences you've had in your day of travel."

Because W wants that interaction to be sincere, cast members are not required to memorize scripted dialogue for dealing with the guest. Since they don't wear nametags (unlike employees in many hotels), it's their responsibility to introduce themselves to the guests and begin to create a positive experience: "How was your travel day? Is there anything we can do to improve your day?" "Some guests just want to be left alone. That's why we don't have use a script; it can sound insincere," explained Limberg.

In employee orientation, which W calls "WOW" training, Limberg stressed, "We need to look for what we have in common with one another—on our side of the desk and the customer's side of the desk. You make people feel comfortable by engaging them in conversation. A good way to do that is to find something that you have in common. We train and educate our people to be comfortable having conversations with anyone and everyone who comes through the doors. We want our guests to feel that this place is different in a very positive way."

FirstMerit: Provide a Consistent, Pleasing Experience

FirstMerit Bank tries to project that same positive attitude when customers visit any one of their 177 branches in northeastern Ohio. Stationed at the front door of every branch is a receptionist whose primary purpose is to greet customers as they come in and offer assistance for whatever matters the customers need to resolve. "By having a receptionist right out there in front, establishing eye contact, there is no question in the customers' mind as to where to go to get their questions answered," stated chairman and CEO John Cochran.

The interior of a FirstMerit branch does not conjure up the typical branch bank experience. The hues are bright, the chairs are comfortable, the displays for banking products are colorful. The teller line is located at the back of the branch so that customers walk past the product displays and the people who are selling those products. Partitions provide privacy for customers who want to conduct their business with their personal FirstMerit banker.

"Our philosophy is that we want to emulate the whole Nordstrom interior feel of nice furnishings and finishes so that people feel that they are doing their business in a vibrant way with a company that invests in itself," Cochran explained. "We have mystery shoppers shop our branches 16,000 times a year to make sure that our people follow our protocol of greeting, serving, and thanking the customer for business. We think we can differentiate ourselves from our competition by providing our customers with a consistent, pleasing experience."

Mike's Express Carwash: Entertain the Customer While Providing Service

A pleasing experience of an entirely different sort is what Mike's Carwash tries to give to its customers. Each of the 19 units in the Indianapolis, Indiana-based chain sits on an acre-plus of highly landscaped property, which is maintained by constant lawn care and an underground sprinkling system. The place doesn't even look like a carwash. The handsome brick and glass buildings sometimes fool people into thinking that Mike's is actually a restaurant. Crews work constantly to maintain the cleanliness of the operation. "We are in such an impulse-driven business," said Jerry Dahm, Mike's vice president, "We have to have that nice clean image from the street."

Unlike the average carwash, Mike's is known as a place that entertains its clientele—particularly the children of its clientele. Giant, furry stuffed animals are placed strategically along the path that cars take on their way to getting clean. As kids look out the window of their parent's car, they get to see stuffed versions of Mickey Mouse, Minnie Mouse, Bert and Ernie, Big Bird, and Raggedy Ann, waving back to them.

"We try to take those opportunities—in the drying chamber, for example—for the kids to see something fun," said Dahm, whose father and uncle opened the first Mike's in 1948. "It's kind of a drive-by amusement park. At Halloween, we have a big budget to turn each location into a set with a Halloween theme complete with scarecrows and cornshacks. We try to make it a fun experience." The animals get peoples' attention.

"When I'm out socially and people learn I'm associated with Mike's, nine times out of ten they don't talk about how clean their car is; they talk about the stuffed animals," Jerry Dahm told me. One time, a regular customer, a Fort Wayne OB-GYN, wrote a letter to Mike's about how much his 3-year-old son, Peter, enjoyed going to the carwash. The little boy always asks Tom Mueller, a Mike's manager, when Barney is going to be joining Bert and Ernie.

"Then, one very cold day in November, when Peter rolled down the window to ask about Barney, Tom handed him a Barney puppet," wrote the customer. "Peter was ecstatic. He carries the puppet wherever he goes, and when he's asked, he is quick to say, 'I got this from Tom at Mike's Carwash.' " You can't buy advertising like that. "Kids drive a lot of buying decisions," said Dahm. "And they are future drivers."

Not all businesses can invest in creating such a creatively unique experience, but whatever business you're in, customers will go away with a memory of the experience.

Kessler's Diamond Center: Create a Place Where People Can Communicate

The first time I met him face to face, Richard Kessler, the owner of the two-location jewelry store in Milwaukee, picked me up at the airport and drove me to a suburban hotel. While I was registering, the young woman at the front desk said to him, "Aren't you Richard Kessler? I just love your store. I got my engagement ring there."

Then we drove over to Kessler's Diamond Center in Greenfield, Wisconsin. It was a late Saturday afternoon in May—prime engagement-marriage-and-anniversary-and-graduation season—and the 2,000 sq. ft. place was packed. It was a beehive of activity; customers were all over the place, either browsing at displays or engaged in deep conversation with salespeople. Soft rock music was playing over the sound system. Small children were busy in their own world in a small play area, which freed their parents to concentrate on the diamonds. Although the scene sounds chaotic, it wasn't. In fact, it was a strangely relaxed atmosphere.

A salesman brought over a newly engaged couple to meet Richard. The young man shook Richard's hand and said, "You have one great store, here. It's so comfortable." After the pleasantries, the couple began to leave, but the man stopped for a moment. His ears perked up to the music on the sound system, and he said to his fiancée, "Wait, I want to hear the end of this song." When the song was over, the couple headed happily out the door.

Later, I told Richard, "This is such a perfect picture. Did you pay all these people to say these nice things? The woman at the hotel—was she a plant? I feel like I'm in the middle of the movie, "The Truman Show." Richard assured me that it was all on the level.

Both of the Kessler Diamond Centers (the other one is in Menomonee Falls) are inviting places to be. In the Greenfield store, the main selling area is a six-sided circle that creates semiprivate nodes—separated by display cases—where salespeople can communicate with customers. Although different sets of customers are only a few feet from each other, they can't hear each other talk because the strategically placed music speakers are designed to play over the separate conversations. An architect, who is a long-time Kessler's client and who knows what the diamond-buying experience should be like, designed the stores. By creating that aura of privacy, Kessler's creates a comfortable setting for that to happen.

Concepts Worldwide: Create a Movable Inviting Place

Concepts Worldwide is one of the top meeting management companies in the United States. The San Diego, California, company puts on meetings, retreats, trade shows, and exhibits for clients all over the world. Unlike the other companies cited in this book, Concepts Worldwide creates an inviting place wherever their business takes them. It's a challenge to do that when you're using some other company's hotel or convention center.

"We like to create a warm, inviting registration area, rather than a sterile environment that can become a barrier to us and to the event the attendees are participating in," said Terri Breining, founder and president of Concepts Worldwide. The firm has developed a service feature called Concierge Check-In. "Knowing we often have a few attendees who arrive late, we keep the registration desk open later than scheduled, and we make sure we have some snacks available for when they finally arrive." Extra chairs are provided at the registration desk for attendees to sit and relax while Concepts planners review the meeting materials with them.

Breining and her staff often create an on-site business lounge for conference-goers called the "Attendee Club," which is equipped with fax, phone, Internet connections, a variety of newspapers, comfortable chairs, coat check, beverages, a television tuned to CNN, a message center, and a quiet place to conduct business. Smokers are also given a comfortable room of their own. It is important, no matter what your business, to consider all your clientele's needs.

"Although smokers are increasingly treated as outcasts, in one meeting we put together, we knew there was a VIP who was a smoker," said Breining. "We placed an ashtray in an area that allowed smoking and then directed her to it. We made sure this area was visible from the registration desk so that we could stay attuned to her needs."

Breining and her motivated staff will do virtually anything to make sure a client is comfortable. Breining recalled one instance when an attendee arrived late and had forgotten to make a reservation at the hotel which was completely full.

How did Concepts Worldwide handle that one? One of the meeting planners gave her own hotel room to the tardy attendee. Now that's a story worthy of Nordstrom.

KEY WAYS TO PROVIDE
AN INVITING PLACE

How can we expect customers to buy what we're offering when we haven't made them feel comfortable by being attentive to every detail of the experience? Whether your business is bricks and mortar or virtual, stationary or in motion, temporary or permanent, you need to create an inviting place where it's a pleasure to do business.

- Enter your place of business as if you've never been there before. What kind of place have you found? What would you like to change?
- Make your public voice or face a pleasant one.
- Create an atmosphere of helpfulness.
- Create an atmosphere of professionalism.
- Create a place that's clean and attractive.
- Make your guests feel that they are a part of your environment.
- Provide a consistent experience.
- Create a place where people can communicate.

3 Hire Nice, Motivated People

Character and personal force are the only investments that are worth anything.
—Walt Whitman

Okay, you're asking, what company or organization *doesn't* want to hire nice, motivated people? Of course, we all do. But Nordstrom and other great customer-service companies want to hire people who are already nice and already motivated to do a good job *before* they walk through the door to apply for a job.

The qualities that Nordstrom is looking for in its employees couldn't be more basic. First of all, the company wants its associates to be nice. "We can hire nice people and teach them to sell," Bruce Nordstrom likes to say, "but we can't hire salespeople and teach them to be nice." The corollary to that philosophy is "hire the smile, train the skill."

Have you ever been able to take someone who is not inherently nice and make him or her nice? It can't be done. But it's amazing how many times during the course of our day we cross paths with people who deal with the public, but are not nice. They are the public

67

voice or public face of a company or an organization, yet they don't like people. You want to shake them by the shoulders and yell, "Find another line of work! Don't work in a job where you have to deal with people!"

Because Nordstrom assumes that people are best trained by their parents, it provides little in the way of a formalized training program. Salespeople are encouraged to find a mentor and to get out there on the sales floor and figure out how to create their own business. Nordstrom believes the key to good customer service is to hire good people and keep working with them, nurturing them and giving them the tools that they need to succeed.

The company tends not to hire people with previous sales experience because those individuals often have difficulty adjusting to Nordstrom's entrepreneurial style. "We didn't used to feel that way," Jim Nordstrom, the late co-chairman of the company, once told me. "But as time has gone on, we've learned [those with little sales experience] haven't learned to say 'no' to customers, because they haven't worked for anybody else." Nordstrom doesn't want people to say "no," they want people to say "yes" to the customer.

What do you look for in job applicants? Is previous experience in your industry a requirement? Or are you like Nordstrom, where you would rather hire someone who is friendly, someone who is inspired to do a great job just because that's the way that person was raised?

Kessler's Diamond Center, like many of the companies featured in this book, is not necessarily looking for people who have previously worked in their particular industry. Bill Aberman, who manages one of the two Kessler stores in Milwaukee, said,

Up until recently, we hired jewelry people. Because we're selling loose diamonds, customers want and need a little more information on our merchandise. But since we have such a different way of doing things, we have found that people with a background in selling jewelry sometimes need to be retrained. Lots of people can give you a professional diamond presentation. We take a softer approach to selling, while jewelers at most other stores only think about closing the sale. Now that we know we can teach people our business and the way we do our business, we look to hire "people people," who go along with our simple philosophy: "We're here to help you buy."

At Feed the Children, the 130 or so people (more during the last three months of the year), who work under vice president Paul Bigham, generally handle donor relations, specifically donors who give at a higher amount and at a higher frequency level than average. In a corporate, secular world, Bigham's forces would be called account managers or account executives. "We look for people who have good people skills, good multitask skills, and a generous heart. When they come to work at Feed the Children, they have to run on adrenaline because this is a busy place," Bigham explained.

Perhaps more importantly, a person who comes to work at Feed the Children has to have "a commitment to being involved in a nonprofit organization," said Bigham. "It's ministry-based, so there has to be some ministry link at some level. We don't require them to belong to a certain religion. But there has to be a reason (other than a financial one) for an individual to come to work at a nonprofit at a lower rate, at a high work base. We have found that the people who don't have that ministry link will quickly become discontented. They leave in a week, and they've wasted their time and our time."

Continental Airlines: Treat Employees with Dignity and Respect

When Gordon Bethune took over Continental Airlines in 1995, he found a dispirited organization that had been battered by a previous ownership that had played employees off against each other to win. That doesn't work well with teams. "They had been treating each other pretty shabbily," conceded the carrier's chairman and CEO. "How could you be at war with your employees and win?"

The Bethune regime began to turn things around first by "compensating employees fairly and tying their compensation to things that customers value, and treating employees with dignity and respect." In 1996, Continental hired the comedian Rodney Dangerfield—whose famous line is "I don't get no respect"—to participate in an in-house training video "because we were going to learn to treat each other with dignity and respect around here," said Bethune. That was a major step toward treating the customer with dignity and respect. "We needed to treat ourselves the way we were starting to treat customers. If someone is not giving dignity and respect, we call them on it and it just stops them cold. It helps them to think about what they are saying and how they are acting."

This new attitude didn't work for everyone, particularly high-ranking executives who were holdovers from the previous administrations. "At the very beginning, many top people left because they couldn't get with the program," Bethune explained.

Bethune credits Continental's rise to the top-ranked customer-service airline to treating employees with dignity and respect, "because first you have to treat people right, and then they become good employees. We had the same employees here when we were the worst-performing airline as we did when we were selected as the best."

How do you turn around a company that's been in the abyss? "You've got to take it one step at a time, just like you would with children that have been abused," said Bethune. "Take the time to show them trust and confidence. We've been able to do that over a period of time."

In 1999 and 2000, Continental was selected among *Fortune* magazine's "100 Best Companies to Work for in America," joining Southwest Airlines as the only two carriers in that elite group. "Robert Levering [who put the list together] said he's never seen a company as big as ours, and as bad as we were, get on that list. It just shows that you can change people," declared Bethune. "When we became an on-time airline, the passengers won because they got to Chicago when they wanted to be there. Our guys won because they got home when they were supposed to be home. Life got so much nicer, so they said, 'Gee, this place really is changing.' So, they buy into the idea that this is not just a new deal from the same old deck."

In 1999, Continental received 120,000 job applications for 8,000 job openings. "I asked people why they applied for work at Continental. People want to work for winners. People want to work for the best. The best people will seek you out," said Bethune. "You should look at our reservation center and see how many people we've hired who have disabilities. They are the best employees. They have the best work ethic. They can do a reservationist's job really well." Like many other top customer-service firms, Continental is not necessarily looking for people with previous experience in its industry. "Our new hires don't come out of a cookie cutter. We are reaching out to bring in more diverse people who want to work here. Continental's president didn't have any experience in the airline business. I've got plenty of that. I'm looking for talent."

Mike's Carwash: Invest in the People Who Are Cut Out for Service

At Mike's Carwash, for every 50 people who come in to apply for a job, one might qualify for a second interview, according to vice president of operations Mike Dahm. Because Mike's operation is virtually 100-percent automated, the operations are not as labor-intensive as a normal carwash. Consequently, "We are extremely fussy as to who we hire," Mike Dahm stressed. Just as Nordstrom is not necessarily looking to hire people who have worked for other retailers, Mike's is not necessarily looking for people who have worked at other carwashes.

"We have learned over the years that there are some common denominators among the successful workers that you can spot," Dahm shared. "A lot of it has to do with the way they feel about themselves. When people come to work, if they have a lot of issues they are bringing from home or school, they can't put their heart and soul in a customer-service-driven business. Give me a man or woman with a good attitude. Our work is not for everybody. We're working outside. Some people don't like outside work. It's physical. You're active. You're handling a lot of transactions." Because of the way labor and hiring laws are written, an employer has to be extremely careful as to the kind of questions he asks potential employees in interview situations.

"I like to ask open-ended questions," Dahm explained. "For example, I'll ask, 'Will you share with me whatever you're comfortable sharing, so that I can get to know you better as a person?' Generally, they will talk about their family, their school; things like that. We try to find out as much as we can about how they feel about themselves. And how they feel about waiting on customers. Some people are cut out for service and some people aren't. After you've been doing this as long as we have [more than 50 years as a family-owned business], you know you have a winner when you spot one. And those are the kinds of people we like to invest all of our training in."

Dahm believes that the key to Mike's success has been that "We really do our homework on hiring. We believe in background checks, drug testing, and other pre-employment testing."

Mike's makes a considerable investment in the people the company hires. Before a new associate is ever allowed to deal with a customer, he or she must attend nine hours of classroom instruction in Mike's own company training school. "The majority of that training has nothing to do with washing cars—but it has everything to do with how people like to be treated where and when they spend their money," said Dahm.

Part of the training of new hires includes encouraging them to smile, showing them the correct way to dress when they come to work, and teaching them how to work with others."We have parents who call us up who would like their kids to come to work for us because we can teach them human relations skills that they can use for the rest of their lives," Dahm declared to me in an interview. "We tell the kids: We know many of you aren't going to make this a career, but the two or three or four years you spend with us, you're going to learn how to treat customers and how to work in a team environment, that you can use the rest of your life, regardless of your career."

In learning how to treat customers, associates-in-training are presented with various scenarios of dealing with customers. When things go wrong, how do you handle customers? What happens if a wheel cover emblem is lost during the wash? What if an antenna has been bent? How do you handle scuff marks on the hood of a car? What if a customer is not satisfied that his car has been completely cleaned?

"We try to anticipate anything that could possibly go wrong, so we can use those opportunities to exceed customers expectations so that they go out and become advocates for Mike's Carwash," said Dahm. "When people have a bad experience, we make sure that we execute the solution so well that they become lifetime customers. We feel that when people complain, they are doing us a favor." Dahm's last statement bears repeating: . . . when people complain, they are doing us a favor. When a customer takes the time to point out what you've done wrong, he or she is helping you become a better customer-service company because you've just been handed a valuable lesson. If the customer just said, "The heck with it," and went to your competition, you would never know why you lost the customer and what you need to improve.

A regular customer who had noticed some scuffs and dullness on the hood and roof of his new GMC Jimmy told the manager of the Mike's Carwash in Castleton, Indiana. In a letter, the customer wrote the company that the manager was "very helpful and considerate" and had the customer fill out a claim form. The manager also promised the customer that he would soon hear from Janeese Sarrazin, Mike's customer-service representative. "As promised, Janeese called me at work to tell me that Mike's would take care of everything—and you did! Thank you for restoring my faith in American business and customer service." The letter was signed "A loyal customer."

All it takes to satisfy a customer are nice, motivated people who have the backing of management. No wonder Mike's has consistently been voted Indianapolis's #1 Carwash by the readers of *Indianapolis Monthly* magazine.

FirstMerit: Hire the Personality and the Confidence

"We take a page from Nordstrom: hire the smile and train the skill," declared John Cochran, CEO of First-Merit Corp. The Akron, Ohio-based bank submits all applicants to a special interviewing process by a major testing and polling organization that identifies the kind of men and women who possess the qualities of personality that the bank is looking for in tellers or personal bankers—the primary people who commonly deal face-to-face with people who visit the branches.

"It's not necessary to us that potential hires already understand the fundamentals of the business. We teach them that. What's more important is their personality."

The polling organization conducted interviews with the top 20 percent of FirstMerit's personal bankers and identified the common qualities those men and women possessed, and then they interviewed the bottom 20 percent and found out the qualities that had prevented them from being more successful. The organization then created an indicator that would identify and weed out applicants who probably would not be successful within the organization.

"This mechanism for identifying the kind of people we want to hire, people who have the confidence and personality to sell the kind of broad product line that we offer is not based on skill," explained Cochran. "It's based on an individual's personality, on the quality of their dealings with people and their personal courage. It's been very successful for us in bringing people into the organization as well as hiring people within the organization for promotion into these jobs."

The mechanism, which is called "Perceiver Test" seeks to measure the soft side, the friendliness, of the individual, according to George Paidas, an executive vice president of FirstMerit Corp. as well as the president and chief executive officer for three of the corporation's regions. "If they don't pass that, they don't go any further in the process. We screen them at that level, then follow up with interviews. That's helped us generate a pool of candidates that is more likely to produce the smile. Beyond that, it's getting a sense of the positive side of a customer."

Paidas, who Cochran called "the conscience" of FirstMerit's emphasis on customer service, noted that the bank has been having a considerable amount of success attracting men and women from outside the banking industry.

As we evolve to a more sales-oriented culture, we find that people who have been in the banking industry find it a little more difficult to adjust to that than folks who have been in retail or other businesses where sales are part of the expectation. We've been hiring the smile and sales experience and teaching banking. That's been pretty effective for us.

FirstMerit sent Paidas to the Disney Institute to learn how to put together the bank's employee orientation program, which has been patterned after Disney's. The bank has separated the orientation segment from a separate session where the bank rules and regulations are listed and explained. Paidas describes the first day-long session that includes a tour of the bank's operations center and one of the branches, as "a day for gaining 'heart share.' " Called "First View," the session is an indoctrination into the company from an emotional, psychological, and spiritual focus. Centered on a program of informative videos, "It seeks to explain to the new employee what we're about. We talk about our past [FirstMerit is a product of the mergers of many banks over 150 years] and how we have become one bank. We talk about our core values and our core purpose. Many employees volunteer to come to Akron and talk with the new employees about our core values and the experiences they've had in the company. We like to close the day with a little bit of fun."

Both FirstMerit and Continental have re-created themselves out of disparate (in the case of FirstMerit) and dysfunctional (Continental) cultures by having a clear vision that included hiring the people who would be comfortable in those new cultures, and giving those people the freedom to become winners. The next step is to create the culture a business wants and needs in order to thrive.

W Hotel: Consider the Person
Who Smiles at You

Unlike FirstMerit and Continental, W Hotel is a brand new organization (founded in 1998) that is just beginning to create a corporate culture. But like the others, the brand is "not necessarily looking for people who have previously worked in other hotels," stated Guy Hensley, vice president of W Hotels. "Quite the contrary. Prior experience isn't all that relevant to us for a lot of positions. We're looking for the right people. We can teach them the nuts and bolts, the mechanics of the job, the technical aspects, how to operate a computer system including how to make a bed. Those are all trainable issues. The things that we're looking for are innate. We can't teach them to be nice."

Thomas Martin, who oversees the hiring of personnel for all Starwood properties, pointed out that because the W brand is "trying to create a new experience, we're not necessarily looking for someone who has worked in hotels before. We have discovered that after a person has spent five years in the culture of another hotel—and is ingrained in that environment—it is going to be more difficult for that person to make a transition to this new way of taking care of customers. You might get someone who works at the front desk who doesn't smile, but he can check you into the hotel in 30 seconds. That's not the point; the point is to make this an enjoyable experience for the guest."

Because W thinks that its employees are essentially on stage at the hotel, the company borrows terminology from the theater by referring to its employees as "cast members." Many of these cast members come from fields that, at first blush, seem somewhat removed from the hospitality industry. "Our employees play an important role in the success of the brand," said Martin, W's Casting Director. "That's why we call our employees cast members." When W advertises that jobs are available, the mass hirings are labeled "casting calls," and the jobs are described as roles to be played—not on a proscenium stage, but rather a hotel lobby, restaurant, or registration desk. "We are looking for people who enjoy the opportunity to have a stage and an audience to perform in front of. The best cast members come to us with an innate desire to please other people and to get their approval. We also like people who have experience in other industries such as retail, because they have learned how to take care of other people."

When W has a casting call, Martin closely observes the behavior of the potential candidates while they are standing in line waiting to be interviewed. "I like to see who smiles," offered Martin. "If someone smiles, I'll watch the person go through the casting call. We have found that the kind of person who is naturally smiling and alert turns out to be a good service provider. Much of our decision making is really visual. How does that individual react during the process?"

Guy Hensley describes the hiring as a three-step process. The first phase is intended to make sure the applicant possesses good communication skills as well as all the basic qualities that are required to work for the hotel. The second phase is finding out whether the applicant is service-oriented, and the third phase is determined by how well that person reacts under the inevitable pressure that comes with trying to satisfy the constant needs of hundreds of guests at one time.

W goes to great lengths to accomplish those essential goals, said Tom Limberg, general manager of the W Seattle:

> *Our application process is a little more drawn out for the applicant than probably any place they've ever applied before. We work with the Gallup organization, which has put together a tool that we use to facilitate the screening and interviewing process. We have a series of questions that speak to themes within people that we feel shows—based on how they answer the question—how they feel and how they think about things like tidiness and neatness and teamwork and customer service.*

Because W is a new hotel brand—the first one opened in New York in December 1998—and is expanding rapidly across the country, the chain is taking an aggressive approach to the tasks of hiring, training, and getting people on the floor ready to do the job, under the fastest possible circumstances. This approach has been severely tested because W has been hiring hundreds, sometimes thousands, of workers at a time when the labor market has been tight in the cities that the chain has selected for expansion sites.

When the W San Francisco was about to open, the hotel received applications from over 2,800 people and hired about 9 percent. By contrast, in Seattle, where the unemployment rate is infinitesimal, 1,000 people interviewed for 300 jobs in July 1999.

"In three days, we hired 250 people; it was terrifying," recalls Limberg. "At the end of the three-day exercise of interviewing, we were within 40 or 50 of the goal of people we wanted to work with us. We found people with incredible professionalism. Most of the people we hired were currently employed; nearly all of them had to provide two weeks notice. Although we would have preferred to hire them immediately—because we were ready to go—the fact that most of those people already had jobs was a good thing. It reinforced the idea that we were hiring the right person. You wait for good people who want to work for you. I'd much rather have nobody than a no-good body."

Limberg has found that the hotel has attracted "tremendous people from within the industry. But we've also taken the risks and have gotten incredible results from being willing to go with our heart and say 'Let's hire the right person and let's work toward the skill set' and not vice versa."

Where do these "tremendous people" come from? When it identifies a new market, the hotel dispatches an army of recruiters that comb the city and scout out potential employees. "If we get tremendous service in a place, we let that person know who we are, how impressed we are," said Limberg.

USinternetworking: Hire People Who Interact with Other People

Although USinternetworking, the software Applications Service Provider to corporations is in a business that is much more technical than the hotel industry, the company takes a hiring approach that is remarkably similar to W Hotel and other companies that are emulating the Nordstrom way.

USi hosts software applications for corporations and delivers them to users over the Internet. It has grown from essentially 11 employees in April 1998 to more than 1,400 by mid-2000.

"We look for people who are very personable and who have the experience," explained John Tomljanovic, Vice President of Client Care. "Because the Application Service Provider industry is virtually brand new, USi couldn't very well find people with experience in the job. I'm from Andersen Consulting. Eight to 10 people followed me here. I have a lot of Big Five accounting folks on the team. Because we look for people who have a background in some of the products that we have to offer, some of our people come from the companies that make the products that we offer, from companies such as PeopleSoft Inc., Microsoft Corp., and Siebel Systems Inc. So, they have that expertise in the products."

Like all companies that aspire to customer-service greatness, USi looks for people who make the client Number One on their list. "We want people who interact well with people," said Tomljanovic. "Plus, we want people who come across in the hiring interview as polite and friendly. The reason why people on my staff joined USi Client Care is because of the way we tailor our support to our clients. That's a huge attraction to the people who are here. Many of them come from environments where the customer support end of things was viewed almost as a necessary evil as opposed to the way we view it." This philosophy of customer service begins with the ideas and commitment of Christopher McCleary, founder and chief executive officer of USi. In a July 26, 1999, cover story in *Forbes* magazine, entitled "The E-Gang: The New Digital Entrepreneurs," McCleary was quoted as saying: "This is our thesis: Forget how any business model operates today. Instead, let's ask what would our customer most desire?"

USi is paid a flat fee for running the in-house software system of clients ranging from the Franklin Covey training and education company to Hershey Foods Corporation, USi is paid only when the system works. It guarantees its clients that USi will keep the system up and running and that it will fix anything that goes wrong at no extra cost. To make money in a situation like that, USi has to have totally dedicated customer-service people.

"The entire company was founded on the idea that you could change the architecture to improve client service," McCleary told me. "When we started the company, it was with one employee, no office, no data center, no bandwidth, no clients. We took three case studies from my previous employer, Digex, and we asked how can we eliminate down time and how can we create higher client satisfaction. Forget the costs for right now. Forget how much money it takes to invest to get this done. How would you do it?" Because USi started out with a clean slate, the company was able to reduce its one and only mission to one simple sentence: To make network applications run better and create higher levels of client satisfaction.

McCleary feels that the typical philosophy in his industry has been not to improve service to customers but rather to generate income with value-added services. "We don't use the term 'value-added' around here because the value proposition we have is the core service offering. It was built from scratch to provide better levels of service. We have created a product out of

providing software as a service. We are a technology en-
abler." And to attract and keep its motivated, customer-
centric staff, USi offers some interesting perks at its
offices by the harbor in Annapolis, Maryland. Employee
benefits include the use of six powerboats and four jet
skis, sailing lessons offered several times a week, a
pizza lunch each Thursday, potentially lucrative stock
options, bonuses, tuition reimbursement, and even in-
line skating. No wonder the magazine *Inter@ctive Week*
selected USi as one of its Top Companies to Work For in
digital communications.

St. Charles Medical Center:
Involve Team Members in the Interviewing and Hiring Process

St. Charles Medical Center in Bend, Oregon, draws
its staff from three counties—Deschuttes, Crook, and
Jefferson—covering about 25,000 square miles and a
population of 150,000. With that small a pool of qualified people to choose from, recruiting becomes particularly crucial at an institution that wasn't leveraging its
most valuable asset, its employees, according to chief
executive officer Jim Lussier.

"We started really talking to every applicant," said
Lussier. "There is a pre-application process before they
even apply for a job. We cut to the quick. We ask them:
What's your mission in life? Why are you in health
care? Why do you want to work at St. Charles? We
asked ourselves if that applicant's aspiration for how
she wants to perform her profession match what we
need in an employee? We try to make clear to any new
applicant that this is a different environment from what
you would find normally. We are certainly interested in

your clinical skills, but you have to bring those other people skills and the ability to work in a team setting, as well as be motivated by all the right things to be able to work at St. Charles."

Applicants are also interviewed by members of the team in which they are going to work, so the team members have a say in whether that new person will fit in. No matter what your business is, it makes sense for more than one person to be making the decision.

"The environment in which we place patients is largely determined by the human staff that we have, and it is augmented by the physical environment. But it's the human staff that's the real turnkey," Lussier emphasized.

In health care, we used to hire anybody who was a warm body. If you had a RN degree or were a good lab technician or whatever and could carry out that clinical work, that's who we hired. Today, we're saying: "That's not it." We can teach virtually anybody the technical skills. It's the motivational stuff. It's being able to be an adult, handle your own conflicts, work in a team setting.

St. Charles finds that it must constantly retrain its staff to work as a team. "There is obviously high stress in health care," said Lussier. "It's real easy for a nurse to get dictatorial because he or she sees the doctor being dictatorial. All of those things have got to change. That really means constant training. We've done that. We've got a program called People-Centered Teams that is about relationship training. The kind of service that we provide is relationship-centered. It's the relationship we establish with patients, with families, and between each other, that ultimately determines the clinical outcome of patients."

Lussier often uses this example: "If you're going into our surgery room to have your head cut open and have a craniotomy done, would you rather have it done by a team that is fully functioning, that gets along well, that supports each other, and is there for the patient, or one that is constantly arguing, bickering, with complex and distracting personal lives? Which person or group do you think will work better clinically?"

Creating that kind of environment is done in a variety of ways. As an example, Lussier cited a staff member, who administers EKG tests. That person and a colleague were trying to do an EKG on a chronically ill child who had been coping with heart defects since her birth.

"They were having a devil of a time getting a good EKG done," Lussier recalled. Nothing was working. "Finally, they sat down with her and sang, 'Twinkle, Twinkle Little Star' for a couple of minutes. It worked. They calmed her down, made her feel comfortable, and were able to perform the process. When they were finished, she was happy as a lark. She wasn't forced into a situation that would make her uncomfortable." That's teamwork.

For the past several years, St. Charles Medical Center has been selected by *Oregon Business Magazine* as one of the top employers to work for in the state and, Lussier said proudly, as a consequence, "We have lots of people applying for jobs and waiting around for years to come here to work."

Concepts Worldwide: Mentor Unselfishly

Concepts Worldwide, the meeting planning company in San Diego, California, tries to hire people with previous meeting-planning experience, "because people hire us as professionals," declared President Theresa Breining. But that's not the sole requirement for becoming a part of the team at Concepts Worldwide, which produces some 200 meetings a year all over the world.

"In the hiring process, we rely heavily on gut instinct, and whether or not we like the person and whether or not other people will like this person," Breining told me. "We have looked at a lot of people who are highly qualified, who look great on paper, and who can technically do the job—but we won't have them work here because they don't fit, because they're not nice. We're not going to have people beating up on other people. So, we've turned away people who have looked good and who are probably working somewhere else for another meeting-planning company."

The Nordstrom approach of "hire the smile, train the skill" has long been Breining's philosophy, "and we've carried that through with huge success," said Breining. "A lot of the people who we have on staff have started with us as interns. They didn't know much [about the business], but were bright, nice, motivated people that wanted to be here. Wanting to be here is a huge factor for us. Fortunately, we have a reputation for being a nice place to work. So, we do have a good pool of people to choose from. But if somebody doesn't want to work here, I will encourage them not to."

Breining's description of her company being "a nice place to work" is not just her opinion; it's the opinion of her employees as well. In 1999, Concepts Worldwide was selected as "Best Company to Work For in San Diego," in a competition sponsored by the Ken Blanchard Companies and the *San Diego Business Journal*. Her employees nominated Concepts Worldwide for the award, and Breining never saw what they wrote about the company until the award was announced.

At Concepts Worldwide, hiring is always, to some degree, a group process. "The degree to which it is a group process depends on who it is and what the position is," said Breining. Because employees work together in teams, when the company is hiring someone, the members of the team who will be working with that individual are involved in the interview process. (The initial screening is done by the company's director of Human Resources.)

Breining feels that it is extremely valuable for potential new employees to talk with current employees. "We want them to know what the real story is here, and they're going to get it from the staff, rather than just from me or the Human Resources person. We also want to get the staff reaction to them."

One necessary quality is being able to "check your ego" when it comes to work. "Whether it is a senior or junior staff member, all staff pitch in with a variety of tasks," said Breining. "We have a culture where our staff can admit their own faults, praise others for good work, and share in the company's objectives."

Concepts emphasizes the value of "mentoring unselfishly," said Breining. "There has been a philosophy from the beginning that this is an organization where people can learn and grow personally and professionally. So, we take on an awful lot of people—and always have—who are motivated, have a great attitude, and want to do the job."

In writing about Concepts Worldwide for the "Best Company to Work For" competition, Sommer Tiffany wrote about her job interview with Terri Breining. After going through a lot of job interviews, being asked what she planned to do with the rest of her life, and being tired of telling interviewers what she thought they wanted to hear, Tiffany "told Terri the truth—that I did not yet have the pleasure of knowing 'what I wanted to do with my life.' Rather than the condemnation that I expected, Terri responded with respect for my honesty and the words that made me accept the position that I currently hold: 'I sincerely hope your future is here with us. If it isn't, if I am able to help guide you into your chosen career, then I have done my job as a mentor.'"

Callison Architecture: Hire People Who Are Excited about Coming to Work

Callison, like Concepts World, also divides its employees into teams. The company looks for people who are self-motivated and team oriented, which, according to Stan Lacgrcid, a principal with the firm, is the ideal combination. "Ultimately, I look at people and ask: 'When they get up in the morning, arc thcy excited about coming to work? Are they excited about being involved in the kind of projects that we are involved in?' If they are, then they will be a good fit."

M.J. Munsell, another principal in the firm, agreed that the team approach is important at Callison, but conceded that being part of a team "might be a turn off to some people. Chances are, you're not going to come here and be a star. You're going to come here and be part of a team and the team is going to be given credit for a successful project. We're not going to put a single person on a pedestal."

Because it is in such a specialized business, Callison looks for people with previous architecture and design experience, but beyond that, the firm carefully looks for the kind of people who will be comfortable functioning within the culture.

"When we screen people, we look for people who are talented, and that talent may come in many forms," said Robert Tindall, president and chief operating officer. "We have to feel like they are going to fit. You want to have similarities [with other employees], but, at the same time, we are looking for diversity. We want them to fit, but we don't want to say 'you have to fit into a particular mold.' We want to bring in diversity to challenge us, to give us different viewpoints, different backgrounds, different educations, different skill bases."

Beyond the obvious skills necessary to do the job, "They have to have similar values," added Tindall. "If they have lower values or higher expectations that can't be achieved, there is going to be conflict. That tends to get in the way of efficiency and good work. We look at people's ability to make good judgment calls. We don't want to be standing over their shoulder and questioning everything that they are doing. If you see that people have good judgment, you're going to let them go."

The principals of Callison have found that good employees come in lots of different packages with lots of different skills. Consequently, there is no one way of achieving success at the firm. "This is a firm where there is not a clear stair-step up to success. We don't have real firm role descriptions for each category of professional. It's sort of an open chart for people. That's real appealing for some people; not appealing for others," said Munsell. "Most of the people can carve out their own career and their own direction in the firm. Typically, we look for people who are entrepreneurial. You do need a technical architect who is very happy sitting down and doing a very detailed set of drawings. But we also look for an aspect of leadership. We want people who are independent, who are comfortable navigating through a system that says, 'if you do this, this, and this, you will reach this level, and so on. You can go from one point to another if you want, if you have the interest in doing that.' "

As its business evolves, Callison has been moving "from serving the client in tangible ways to more intangible ways, such as providing the ideas for the clients. It's a challenge for our staff, who are trained to be artists and architects, to think like businesspeople and idea people," said Laegreid. "The whole aspect of providing ideas is one way we've evolved our customer service."

Realty Executives of Nevada: Ask Lots of Questions

Realty Executives faces a much different challenge when it comes to attracting nice, motivated people because all the people hired are experienced agents, who are independent contractors. Agents, who earn their money through sales commissions, pay Realty Executives a fixed management fee of $350 per month and a fixed transaction fee of $350 per closing that covers a variety of services, including continuing education, broker support, broker management, attorney services, and the rent on the office building.

These independent contractors must uphold their own reputation, as well as that of Realty Executives. Consequently, "We are going to ask a lot of questions in the interview about their source of business, and their professionalism and ethics," said Fafie Moore, co-owner of the firm, who has found that "Our reputation has helped our recruiting."

"I'll ask, 'What are you looking for in a company? What are you looking for in a manager?' " added Moore "After I have a feel for what you're looking for, I'm going to explain to you how Realty Executives is going to help meet those needs for you. If you say things that tell me that you don't have the same [ethical] guidance system that we do, I'm probably going to suggest that this is not the place for you, because that's not the way we do things. If you ask if you are allowed to do certain contractual things that we don't feel comfortable doing, that's a red flag for me."

Another red flag starts waving when an agent badmouths previous employers or coworkers. "If you tell me that your last broker was a bozo, and then I find out that you've gone through three brokers in the last three years, and they are all bozos, I know that it's just a matter of time before I get on the bozo list," she quipped.

Moore said that it could take a long time to recruit an experienced agent who will fit comfortably into the Realty Executives culture. (She cited a couple of current agents who moved to Realty Executives after a year of talking.) "An experienced agent, who has a quality business, is reluctant to pick up and move because that move is going to impact all of her clients. She wants to make sure that you have the reputation that she wants to associate with. And she wants to know what benefits she can pass on to their clients."

Jeff Moore, Fafie's husband and partner, emphasized how important it is for agents who work together to like each other. "The attitude of the individual is just as important as their skill level," he said. "You can teach somebody the mechanics of being a salesperson, but you can't change the attitude."

KEY WAYS TO HIRE NICE, MOTIVATED PEOPLE

What do you look for in an employee—a warm body or someone who can take over when you're not around? Virtually every great customer-service company is looking for nice, motivated, energetic, entrepreneurial people because those people are the building blocks that go into creating a company where customer service is paramount:

- Previous experience in your industry should not be the determining factor in hiring.
- Hire people who enjoy people and who are excited by the job.
- Hire the smile, train the skill.
- Hire the personality and the confidence.
- Hire people who share your values.
- Involve potential coworkers or team members in the interview and hiring process.
- Treat employees with dignity and respect.
- Invest in the people who are cut out for service.
- Mentor unselfishly.

 Sell the Relationship: Service Your Customers through the Goods and Services You Sell

> *A salesman minus enthusiasm is just a clerk.*
> —Harry F. Banks

Patrick McCarthy is Nordstrom's all-time top salesperson. Until he retired in early 2000, after 29 years with the company, Pat was the quintessential Nordstrom employee. For the last 25 of those years, Pat sold men's tailored clothing in the downtown Seattle store, and was Number One in sales throughout the chain for an astonishing 20 years in a row. He was undoubtedly the most famous salesman in Seattle. Drawing from a personal client list of 7,000—from recent graduates to United States senators—he racked up well over $1.5 million in sales every year.

Pat tells the story of playing golf one day with a couple of people who didn't know who he was. At the first tee, one stranger who was in his foursome asked the typical question: "What do you do for a living?" To which Pat replied: "I sell a relationship."

The questioner looked at Pat kind of funny, and returned to the golf game. But at the second hole, he had to ask the question again: "No, really, what do you do for a living?" Pat replied: "I sell men's suits at Nordstrom."

"Oh, so that's what you do," said the stranger, fully satisfied with the answer.

"No," Pat replied. "That's not what I do. What I do is I sell a relationship." And that's exactly what you are doing in your business: Selling a relationship. People like to do business with people they like. If your product or service is similar to your competitor's and the price for that product or service is in the same ballpark, what's going to get you the business and not your competitor? I submit it's the relationship you have with your customer; the trust you have built up over time. Once you've established that relationship, why should your customer go anywhere else?

McCarthy's first indication of the value of selling the relationship came when he first joined Nordstrom in 1971 and saw how Ray Black, the company's most successful men's clothing salesman, had made a living out of the relationships he had with his customers. Black taught McCarthy the value of remembering names: He could remember not just a person's name, but also his last purchase. "Ray was businesslike, focused, very sharp, and witty," McCarthy said. "He was very low key and not pushy. He made suggestions and gave customers choices. I never saw anyone go out of there displeased. People would come in asking for him. If he wasn't working that day, they would leave and come back on a day when he was working."

McCarthy's best friend at Nordstrom was Pat Kennedy, who, until his retirement in 1999, oversaw the men's shoes division, which represented about a quarter-billion-dollar business. Year in and year out, Kennedy's division had the best financial performance—the best profit margins, the fewest returns; you name it—of any other division in the Nordstrom chain.

Someone once asked Kennedy what he instructed the salespeople in his division to do to get those kinds of results. His answer: "I tell them to measure both feet."

Measure both feet? In the literal sense, a knowledgeable shoe salesperson will measure both feet because she knows that a customer's right foot might be a slightly different size than the left foot. So, by measuring both feet, she is showing her customer that she knows about that potential size difference. But, even more important, while she's measuring both feet, she's taking the time to talk to the customer and to begin to plant the seeds of a relationship. She's taking advantage of the extra time to ask questions: What kind of business are you in? Are you on your feet all day? Do you need dress shoes or more casual shoes? Do you play sports? All the while, that salesperson is creating a relationship. What do you do in your business to create a relationship? When it comes to customers, new and old alike, how do you—metaphorically speaking—measure both feet?

Continental Airlines develops its relationship with passengers through its frequent flyer program, called One Pass, which was selected in 1997 through 1999 as the best airline elite program, according to an award sponsored by MCI/American Express *Skyguide/Inside Flyer* magazine. (To qualify for Silver Elite status, one must fly 25,000 miles in a calendar year or 30 flight segments; for Gold Elite, 50,000 miles or 60 segments; and Platinum Elite, 75,000 miles or 90 segments.) The program consistently wins for Best Overall Customer Service, Best Program Newsletter, Best Web Site, and Best Travel Specials.

"One Pass Elite members are our best customers," Bethune emphasized. "We work really hard to reward and care for our best customers. You have to cater to those repeat business customers. By default, if you are doing a good job for them, you are doing a good job for the guy who has just tried you for the first time. For the Platinum Elite, we'll kiss their tail, and pay attention to what they want. People like the fact that we anticipate what the customer thinks, not just act on what we think. That's how you maintain a relationship with your customer."

Relationships are perhaps even more important for small mom-and-pop retail operations, which these days are often described as "a dying breed." One small independent retailer who has fought back is New London Pharmacy, a 4,000-square-foot shop on Eighth Avenue, in the heart of Manhattan, which battles a dozen competitors—including several major chains—within a half-mile radius.

The owners of New London did a lot of necessary things, such as cutting prices 10 percent or more on their top 200 best-selling drugs, changing its product assortment, including an emphasis on homeopathic remedies. All those moves helped, but what separates the store from its competitors is the relationship it has with its customers. On a typical day, manager Jimmy McGee acknowledges regular customers by their names; an employee happily runs off copies for an elderly patron; another employee will explain how to program a universal remote. If a customer can't pick up his medication by the time the store closes at 7:30 PM, the pharmacist will leave it at the restaurant next door. In 1998, the co-owners, John and Abby Fazio hired a fourth pharmacist, which freed up all of the store's pharmacists to have more time to speak with customers about their medicine—because their doctors didn't have the time. A

New London customer summed up her feelings about the store to a *Wall Street Journal* reporter: "No question is too minute, no product is too small for them to take the time to help. It's a community place. How could I not support this?"

Do you take the time to maintain the relationship with your customer?

Kessler's Diamond Center: Seek to Understand the Customer First

In 1991, Richard Kessler, then 38 years of age, had been running his business for 11 years. The first few years, the business had gone very well, with consistent gains. But in recent years, sales had flattened out, and he was becoming increasingly dissatisfied with the direction his company was taking.

Then Kessler spent a weekend at a seminar presented by Anthony Robbins, the famed motivational speaker, and left with a change in his belief system. "At that time, we were the smallest jeweler in the city of Milwaukee," Kessler recalled. "I always believed that some of these bigger names in town were just invincible; they were Goliaths. But after the Tony Robbins experience, I realized that they were not that big; the problem was my belief system. I analyzed what my life is about and what serving the customer means. So, my vision became, 'I want to be the most respected name in diamonds in southeastern Wisconsin,' and that has been our vision ever since."

Kessler asked himself: What was it going to take to achieve that goal? The first thing, he realized, was how his people related with customers. "Our criteria was this: What if it's 11 o'clock on a Saturday morning, and we've got a store full of customers and a customer comes in and says, 'My diamond fell out.' What would you do in front of all these other customers? Well, you'd fix it. Then, why wouldn't you do the same thing at 2 o'clock on a Tuesday, when there's nobody in the store? If you're really here to serve the customer, you would do it then, as well," said Kessler.

Operating in a business where the competition will sell a customer a diamond engagement ring and then charge for tightening it a couple of months later, Kessler made it a policy that his store would never ever charge a customer to repair a piece of jewelry. He declared: "When you buy that piece of jewelry, that's the last time you put any money into it."

Doesn't that cost him money? And how does he explain that philosophy to his employees? Kessler says:

Like Nordstrom, we take the long-term view of every-thing we do, whether it's hiring a new employee, buy-ing a piece of equipment, making a piece of jewelry, or establishing a relationship with a customer. We're not looking to make one ring sale. We know that the customer has long, long-term value, which is much greater than this one sale. If we were only going to focus on that thousand-dollar ring I sold you, and then I do something to mistreat you that ends our re-lationship, then the whole process was worthless to begin with.

Like Nordstrom, Kessler's Diamond Center has lots of wonderful stories of customer service above-and-beyond the call of duty that ultimately solidify relation-ships with their customers.

"We've had instances where people have been in au-tomobile accidents and wound up in the emergency room at the hospital where their jewelry had to be cut off, and they bring it back to us with tears in their eyes and ask, 'Now what am I going to do?' We tell them: 'You'll have to wait until Friday so I can make you a new one.' "

Bill Aberman, who manages one of Kessler's two stores, said that part of building a relationship is to "Seek to understand the customer first. What is their agenda? They will tell you what they need. Trust is what enables us to sell to the customer."

Today, Kessler's is the biggest jeweler in Milwaukee, and Richard eventually hopes to expand the operation from two to six stores, with the goal of becoming the largest jeweler in southeastern Wisconsin.

Keith Moro, a Kessler's salesman, likes to tell the story of a customer, who came into the store after his car had been broken into. The thieves took his CD player, as well as a 14-karat gold rose, which is a Kessler trademark in the Milwaukee area. He had come into the store to buy another gold rose for his girlfriend for Christmas. Moro gift-wrapped it and then told the customer that the rose he had just purchased was free, compliments of Kessler's. Don't you think that gesture not only made that customer's Christmas, but also renewed his faith in his fellow man? That's how you build a relationship beyond just selling someone a product.

Concepts Worldwide: Spoil the Client Whenever Possible

Jaime Rosales, a meeting planner with Concepts Worldwide, had done a series of meetings all over the world with the project leader of a major account. One particular meeting was being held in Barcelona, Spain, a city that the client/project leader had never before visited. Jaime knew that his client was celebrating a birthday and decided to cook up a little something special.

There was an extra free day in Barcelona, where they had no professional obligations, so Jaime arranged for his client a surprise birthday train ride of the scenic Spanish countryside, complete with a cake and a bottle of champagne.

"Not only was it a wonderful surprise for the client, but it was also a positive for our planner because he got to know this client better on a personal level," said Terri Breining, CEO of Concepts Worldwide. Jaime didn't have to ask permission to put together the surprise. He got the idea, ran it past a Concepts Worldwide executive back at the office, and put the whole thing together because he genuinely liked this client, who, coincidentally, gives the company a lot of business. "As a result, we have been able to sustain with that client a really great relationship that remains strong to this day," said Breining.

Knowing the birthday of a client is part of Concepts Worldwide's philosophy of creating a relationship by sweating the small stuff. "We look into the details of our clients—preferences, favorite foods or drinks, dislikes, and so on—so they can be spoiled whenever possible," said Breining. "We generally don't have clients fill out forms. Instead, we ask our people to pay attention and to make notes of those kinds of things. We notice what they order and what they're drinking; any special requests that they have made and so on. They are generally surprised when we know, but it's really just a matter of paying attention and responding.

To Breining, those are the kinds of efforts that are necessary to build relationships. "Our clients depend on the relationships they form with our staff," she said. "Many of our clients become very attached to their favorite planners and insist on their services again and again." That kind of personal relationship is crucial in every business.

Realty Executives of Nevada: Track Your Sphere of Influence

The real estate business in the white-hot Las Vegas market, is one of the most competitive in the country. For Fafie and Jeff Moore and their team, most of the business comes as a result of referrals through relationships with coworkers, neighbors, and friends because "That's where the client's greatest comfort is," Fafie told me.

"One good referral can generate four or five sales," said Jeff. "That represents the lifetime value of the client. For an agent who can gain the respect and trust of the customer, the lifetime value of that one customer could represent a significant annual income each year. One customer can account for hundreds of thousands of dollars of income—if it's handled correctly. You only need a handful of foundation customers that can spread to bigger customers. In real estate today, when an agent retires, he sells his "book of business." Years ago, industry members just walked out of the business and everybody was left on their own; there was no residual value for your effort. Today, if you've built name identity, a reputation for customer service, and the foundation of relationships, those important connections are worth a lot of money. With data-based contact-management systems, we can document who we sold the house to, and who recommended us, so it's easy for you to see the commission stream that was created by a sale to that one satisfied client. You'd be amazed at how many agents sell a house and never contact that client again."

In an effort to build relationships, Realty Executives asks its agents to track their "spheres of influence"— satisfied clients who would recommend their services— and to keep in regular contact with those people, because you never know when that relationship might lead to a sale.

To illustrate the point, Fafie Moore pointed to a personal experience back when she and Jeff were selling real estate in Phoenix, before they moved to Las Vegas. A client told the Moores about friends who were moving from St. Louis to Phoenix, and needed help locating a rental. The husband was a plastic surgeon, the wife a dentist.

"When I called up the people, they told me they were already working with another agent," Fafie recalled. "I asked them when they were coming to Phoenix, and what day they were meeting the agent. They were coming in on Friday but could meet the agent only on Sunday because he was a policeman and Sunday was his only day off. I said, 'I'll meet you on Saturday,' which I did. By Saturday evening, they had a rental property. The customer later told me that he knew that he could work with me when I said we could meet on Saturday. A month later, that couple referred me to another couple who was moving to Phoenix."

Jeff Moore offers this truism for any business involved with sales: A referral that comes from a satisfied client is a lot easier to get than new business from a stranger. He has seen many people in real estate miss the importance of relationships because they are too focused on getting the money. "In a service business, it all starts with service," he said.

> *If you get into real estate solely for the money, you will usually hit a wall after about two years in the business because it's not fun anymore. But if you get into real estate because you want to serve the customers and you want to build relationships, the transactions will be a lot easier and that wall will be a lot smaller. If you worry about the needs and concerns of the customer, and not worry about the dollar you can earn, you will find that there will always be more dollars.*

Realty Executives extends that idea of relationships to its independent agents, because the Moores' philosophy is that their customers are the agents who are a part of the company. "We have to satisfy the agents for their needs and wants, so we give them the tools to make money," explained Gail McQuary, Realty Executives' corporate broker, who serves as the company's liaison to the agents. "What we are selling is ourselves and our ability and knowledge of what we are doing. We are selling the relationship."

One of the most successful independent agents working for Realty Executives is a bundle of energy named Laura Worthington, whose business is so good that she has eight people on her staff. To Worthington, her job far transcends selling someone a house. She is there to take care of them every step of the way—even after the paperwork for the house has closed.

"I tell people: 'I'm your real estate consultant for life. If you have questions, I am always accessible. I will help you,'" said Worthington, a busy wife and mother of three who somehow finds the time to help an elderly client with his income tax. "Somebody once said, 'Laura doesn't just sell houses to people, she bar mitzvahs with them.' "

Now, *that's* a relationship.

Mike's Carwash: Create a Lifetime Experience

As a customer, do you ever think about your relationship with your carwash? The people at Mike's certainly want to make sure that you do. "We live and die on repeat business," said CEO Bill Dahm. Dahm's father, Joe, who co-founded Mike's in 1948, used to shake the hand of every customer after the job was done. "We tell our people that we're looking to create a lifetime experience for each and every customer. I don't care if the car looks perfect to you, if the customer doesn't like the job we did, we'll put the car through the wash again. We encourage customers to ask for that if they are not satisfied. If we make a mistake, we make sure that the customer knows we're going to take care of it immediately; not two or three weeks later. They know we're going to stand behind our product. When mistakes happen, it's very important to make sure that customers know you're going to take care of them."

It also helps to have relationships with the right people. When Earl Embry was the assistant manager at a Mike's Carwash in a rough neighborhood of Indianapolis, it was common practice for the closing manager/supervisor to offer free washes to the deputies in the Marion County Sheriff's office, if they hung around until closing.

"One night, we had been fairly steady and I had two other associates closing with me, so I was checking quality, looking over the lot and mopping an occasional car," said Embry. "I heard several loud pops, which at first I dismissed as being a customer setting off fire crackers. After mopping another car, I started wondering if they hadn't sounded more like gun shots. They were indeed. One of our customers had shot someone attempting to steal his car. When I placed the 911 call, I thought a few officers would respond. But I was surprised to see all the deputies and Indianapolis Police Department officers I had come to know respond immediately. After the situation was under control, one of them told me that when they heard a shooting occurred at Mike's Carwash, they were afraid one of our associates had been shot. They could have done their job and left, but the officers took the time to make sure that we were all okay, too."

Callison Architecture: Reinvent Yourself

Callison is not interested in doing a single project with a client and never hearing from them again. "Because our goal is to perpetuate the firm's life, many decisions are based on long-term rather than short-term benefit," Robert Tindall, the president of Callison, told me. "We've had jobs where we could have charged more, but we took the long-term view. I don't want just one project with that one client; I want a dozen projects with that client." Callison employees devote a lot of attention to building up that relationship.

"In our business, the best marketing situation is the call to start the job; not a competition, not a fee proposal," said Tindall. "We will do a lot of things to get the call to start the job and not have to jump through hoops. We hope that the call represents the quality of the relationship that has been built with that client and its long-term reward. If we have done a good job in building that relationship—and bringing the value as well—then our client will find a way to make it happen."

Tony Callison, who founded the firm in 1973, and who set the tone for how all the people who have come after him think and operate, embodied that philosophy. The philosophy of Tony Callison, who passed away in 1988, was carried over and embodied by his successor, David Lindsey, who left the presidency of Callison in 1990 to become vice president and corporate director of store planning at Nordstrom, a position he has held since 1990.

Lindsey's Ten Principles remain the essence of the Callison way:

1. Give the clients more than they expect.
2. Leave them something to remember you by.
3. Think the project (problem) through.
4. Ask yourself: If I were the client, would I pay for this?
5. Don't give reasons why it can't be done. Tell how it can be done and the consequences.
6. Don't wait to do it if it can be done now.
7. Service the client not the project.
8. You don't know if you don't ask.
9. Start a conversation with one new person every day.
10. Sketch ideas being discussed in front of the client. Always bring tracing paper and scale.

Regarding Principle Number 10, Callison executive Stan Laegreid said, "To this day, I never go to a meeting with a client without bringing along tracing paper, so that I can show the client an idea. It doesn't have to be some grand sketch suitable for framing; it just needs to outline your thinking on paper. A lot of times we forget how important that is."

By sketching an idea in front of the client, the client sees how an architect is thinking, and it demystifies the experience. On the other hand, it subtly drives home the point to the client that the architect can do this job, and you, the client, can not.

Part of maintaining any kind of relationship is making sure it doesn't get too stale or too familiar, where you end up losing the chemistry that made the relationship work. To keep it fresh, you have to keep changing, ever so slightly.

"With companies that we've had long-term relationships with, we have to constantly reinvent ourselves so that we don't become lazy and give them what we've always given them. It's a constant challenge. It's easier to grab a new client and wow them. The work begins after a few years when they are thinking, oh, we've been with these guys," said M.J. Munsell, a principal in Callison. "There are a lot of people knocking on our clients' doors. We have to remind ourselves every day that we are in constant competition with those other firms."

To guard against this complacency, Callison has tried several approaches. "One way might mean introducing new people in the firm to the client or providing the client with new services or a new product that they are not expecting from us," Munsell suggested. "It might mean changing the way we present to the client. That's how we invigorate our staff. We tell them: 'Don't just give us the same old thing. What can you do new for this client today that you didn't do for them yesterday?' By tackling this problem, we can have creative fun and do new things in the process."

Bob Tindall reminds his colleagues that ongoing service to a client is not a rubber stamp, but rather a source for new ideas and approaches. Callison devotes a lot of time and energy to researching the industries of their clients and tries to figure out where those industries are going.

"We want to go to our key clients and tell them two or three things that we think are going to be the next trend," said Tindall. "We want to be able to say confidently that in order for the client to go forward, from our point of view, this is the size of the site they need, and this should be the location." Just as Nordstrom salespeople maintain relationships with their customers by sending them thank-you notes after a sale, "We clip out articles on subjects we think our client will be interested in, based on a conversation we had," Stan Laegreid related. "Or we will call a client and say we saw this particular project; we think you need to go see it. And the client we have relationships with will do the same for us."

St. Charles Medical Center: Make Palpable the Difference between You and Your Competitors

All the customer surveys that St. Charles Medical Center takes consistently show that the general public's primary image of hospital-based care is in the form of a registered nurse, because that's the relationship people believe is most important during their hospital stay. Consequently, St. Charles devotes a lot of time talking with patients about how the Medical Center puts together teams and how those teams interact with patients throughout their stay—from the evening emergency room clerk who admits them, to the staff who cared for them during their stay, to the people who facilitated their discharge.

"Ultimately, it's all about relationships," said St. Charles CEO Jim Lussier. "Everybody's got the same basic clinical skills and technology. But it's the relationship experience that's going to determine what you think of this place. So, we try to differentiate ourselves and our services based on that relationship and what people actually experience. And we want that difference to be palpable. We want people to be able to walk in the front door and know that they are in a medical facility that's completely different from any they've ever been in before. We're just like Nordstrom in that patient-to-patient word-of-mouth is going to make or break our reputation."

An overriding theme in St. Charles' employee orientation and training is the idea that the medical center is "a cathedral of healing. We want that same cathedral power in the healing professions that churches have." Said Lussier,

> *That powerful feeling comes about from the relationships patients have with everyone who works for St. Charles. When you walk through the halls, you want people smiling at you. If you appear to be lost and need directions, we want somebody to stop and help you and take you where you need to go. Not only are all of those things a part of our training, they are also implicit in what we're trying to do as an institution.*

Lussier readily admits that St. Charles has a long way to go, and that he and his staff are constantly trying to figure out easier and better ways to take care of the customer and reinforce the relationship. He pointed out that, "Very often, this leads to some battles with physicians because the older physicians think that they—not the patient and the family—should be the center of our attention. There are times when we make something more convenient for the patient that might also make it a little less convenient for the physician, who sometimes takes objection to that."

Lussier believes that customers as a whole are more aware of the small details and features of the institution, rather than the grand ones. "We save lives and we do all those wonderful things, and patients will love us for it, but by and large those are not the primary experience of the majority of our patients," said Lussier. "The majority of our patients are people who come in here, need a good place to park, need happy people helping them out, and really feel like they're the center of our attention while they are here."

FirstMerit: Make a Difference in the Life of a Customer

"At FirstMerit, we start everything with this one basic question: Why do we exist?" said CEO John Cochran. "We feel that our mission at FirstMerit is to improve and preserve the wealth of customers in every contact we have with our customers. We do that through relationship banking."

Cochran conceded that virtually every bank talks about the concept of "relationship banking" as if it were some exotic concept. Indeed, many of them employ people with the title "relationship banker." But FirstMerit's strategy is that every member of its team is involved with the banking relationship with the customer.

"Our strategy for relationship banking is offering customers banking with a personal touch," he explained. Assuming that a company offers its customers a competitive product, the quality that will separate one company from another is an understanding of the customers, "through knowledgeable, caring bankers, who care enough to spend the necessary time to provide solutions that are particularly tailored to individual needs."

Developing a meaningful banking relationship is no different than developing a meaningful emotional relationship because the same core values apply. The first core value is based on trust. "Whatever we do with our customer must be done reliably and with integrity, for the benefit of the customer," said Cochran. "We believe that what we do must stand the test of time—that the customer can count on the fact that we're not going to give him something that's going to blow up on him. We're not going to provide him inconsistent service— we're not going to sell him something and not be able to serve." The second core value at FirstMerit is that individual employees are empowered to make a difference in the customer's life. "Everyone of our people is trained to take control of any customer situation they face. There's nothing that they can't handle," Cochran declared. "We tell them that they can make a difference in the life of the customer they are servicing at this moment."

Finally, FirstMerit is committed to providing service that's significantly better than the competition. "If we can't provide undifferentiated, high-quality service, we will not be able to exist," said Cochran. "Relationship banking is the ability to serve the customer in a differentiated way on a consistent basis."

W Hotel: Read What Customers Want

A frequent guest arrived at the W New York to check in, and asked one of the Welcome Agents behind the registration desk if a particular Welcome Agent—the one who had checked him in on all his other visits to the hotel—was on duty. It was 2 o'clock in the afternoon, and the guest was told that that particular cast member didn't start his shift until 3 o'clock. The guest said, "Then I'll wait in the lobby until 3." The guest had established a relationship, which, for him, had become an essential, comforting ingredient in his W experience.

That Welcome Agent told Thomas Martin, W's Casting Director, that whenever that particular guest checks into the hotel, they always have a warm friendly conversation. "By creating that rapport, our cast member and our guest had established a connection and a trust level," said Martin. "When you're a traveler on the road, that kind of relationship is priceless. You feel less like you're away on the road and more like you're coming home."

The relationship begins when the guest comes through the door of a W Hotel. Doormen and bellmen (called Welcome Ambassadors in the parlance of the W) "need to have enthusiasm for the brand and truly believe in the product," Martin enthused. "They need to talk from the heart—not from a script—about the features of the room as if it was their own home. Customers have to feel like this is their own personal home. That's a cliché that gets thrown around hotels, but I think our staff relates to people on a more personal level just by dropping the formality."

Cast members are encouraged to be sensitive to the needs and moods of the guests and to do whatever it takes to satisfy them. "We want them to go out of their way to read what customers want and to be able to make them comfortable," said Martin. "If we don't have something in the hotel that a customer asks for, we encourage cast members to go out and get it. It could be something as simple as the time when a guest arrived late at night at W Seattle and discovered that he didn't have solution for his contact lenses, which we don't sell in the hotel. A cast member tracked down some solution at an all-night pharmacy in Seattle and brought it to the guest. The guest was floored."

Tom Limberg, general manager of the W Seattle says that developing the relationship is rooted in execution, consistency, and follow-through. Limberg believes that, "The key to everyone's success is how we treat each other and how we treat our customers throughout the entire exercise. It's how you open the hotel, it's how you run the hotel; how you open your business and how you close your business. It has to be consistent day in and day out, year in and year out. In our business, we never close. It's 24 hours a day, 365 days a year. We have to be around to know what's going on firsthand. We need to be around to show that third shift that what they do is important to us. In some businesses, sometimes you can't get a phone answered in the administrative office after 5 o'clock. Maybe you can't find a manager on a weekend. You must make it a priority that the vehicle for service or resolving an issue at a higher level is there That's how you build and maintain a relationship."

USinternetworking: Take Responsibility

Without a deep, trusting relationship with its clients, USi would not be in business. Corporate clients pay USi a fixed fee every month to run and manage a wide variety of software programs—covering every aspect of the client's business, from e-mail to accounting—that are run on USi servers at various sites throughout the country. Clients, such as Liberty Financial, BASF, USWest, and GE Capital can connect to those servers either through the Internet or special telephone lines.

A key to building a solid relationship is taking responsibility. The premise of USi's business is being accountable for every aspect of the client's experience with these software applications. For example, to save its clients from experiencing online traffic jams, USi formed direct-link relationships with Internet providers such as GTE, PSINet, AT&T, UUNet, AGIS, or Sprint. By smoothing out the process, service performance is better.

"That's what this business is about: being client-centric," declared CEO Chris McCleary. "Clients are looking for a company that takes full responsibility for every aspect of the software application because, if anything goes wrong, they want to know who is going to fix it—and when is it going to be fixed."

"When we started this company, the first thing we did was analyze what was going on in our industry," explained Vice President of Client Care John Tomljanovic. "A lot of our competitors and a lot of industry participants have hidden behind the complexity (of the software and the connectivity) as a reason not to offer predictable and consistent levels of service, and not to meet expectations. That's why we assume total responsibility. We also buy the software on behalf of each client, but we don't charge for it up front. We tell the client that in month 6 or month 8 or month 28 of the contract, if you're not receiving your level of service, don't pay the bill until you do. So, we don't get paid unless they're happy. Because we know that much of our revenue gains in the future will come from our existing client base, we know that they've got to be happy; otherwise they won't buy anything else from us. That puts the onus on us to provide the levels of service that support the service level agreements that we have provided. It's unheard of in our industry."

To cultivate relationships, USi account managers are required to make a monthly visit to their clients, and to review the results of that month. "We try not to make it a formal business meeting, but rather a lunch or a golf date," said Tomljanovic. "The idea is that every month the client sees his account manager and has a chance to talk to him. This way, we are reiterating the fact that we're here for you; we're here to take care of you. Clients love it. They tell me that they used to see their old provider once a year. At least once a month, I also visit clients, so that I am presenting a presence as well."

Tomljanovic cited one example when he and a client spent a day playing golf. When the client returned to his office at about 6 o'clock in the evening, he got a page from someone at USi calling to tell him that there were problems occurring with his site. The client called Tomljanovic, who had also just learned of the problem. "Within 10 minutes, we had it resolved," Tomljanovic recalled. "The client said, 'I'm so glad we played golf today. When are we going to do it again?' He didn't underplay the problem and the fact that his company had experienced a little bit of downtime, but he was so enthused about the relationship. People can be very forgiving if you hear the problem and you take care of the problem."

Developing a trusting relationship means that you tell the client the bad news right away. For example, if a client's e-commerce site is running slow, "We see what the problem is internally, and if we think we can fix it fast enough, we don't call the client. That is something that is totally forbidden here," Tomljanovic emphasized. "As soon as we know of everything that could possibly impact the client, we call them first and give them the bad news. We are confident that clients are generally reasonable if they have full information. Even if we have some negative results with regard to the system performance—whether it's our fault or their fault—we come forward with the bad news." USi is constantly driving home the point that the client service provided by its client-care staff is what sets it apart from the competition.

> *We tell our people that the Applications Service Provider marketplace is young. A year or two from now, there are going to be other companies that are going to offer similar solutions. The key to making us different is that we try to support the client better than anybody else. At the end of the day, with these highly complex highly technical solutions, in order to keep customers happy, it really comes down to service.*

One of the ways that founder and CEO Chris McCleary drives home this point is by including his home telephone number on the back of the business card that he gives to clients and vendors alike. He has found that this small gesture "really sets the tone for us in communicating to our clients. For us, taking care of the client is a 24-hour-a-day commitment, including personal time. Interestingly, since I've been doing this for the past five years, clients have called my home only on two occasions—one of those times, they called to say something went right. The impact of that commitment illustrates to a client or a prospect that that's how we run the company."

By building and maintaining relationships with existing clients through the services it sells, USi can potentially sell additional services down the road. "We have seven different product groups," said Tomljanovic. "We don't sell all these product groups all at once. We get one product group in service and then we try to sell another one."

How does USi show employees that it is necessary to take the long-term view in building relationships? "Most of these folks have been in the industry with other companies," said Tomljanovic. "When they do execute their jobs pursuant to the company strategy, and they find they have an exponential number of very happy clients, their reaction is almost one of amazement: 'My gosh, you mean you can make an information technology services client happy?' We show them that when you follow our methodology, you really can have happy clients."

Feed the Children: Thank the Customer for the Relationship

At Feed the Children, donor representatives—the charity's equivalent of account executives—are constantly out in the field visiting people who have donated money and goods to express appreciation for what these donors have done and to acknowledge contributions they have made. "We try to develop personal in-person relationships so that donors can associate Feed the Children with a flesh-and-blood individual," executive vice president Paul Bigham told me. "We want to do more than send them a letter or a receipt. We try to get as close to them as we can. We thank them for what they've done.

We show them that they're respected and appreciated and that they are making a difference."

Quite often, these visits to donors become much more than an opportunity to say thank you. Donor representatives sometimes become deeply involved in the personal lives of the givers, many of whom are generous elderly people of modest means. Some donor representatives have gone out to drugstores to pick up medicine for people who are unable to do so on their own. Some representatives have fixed the living room piano. Others have helped people reestablish contact with estranged family members.

"We are more than happy to do anything that is legal and moral while not overreaching," said Bigham. Not atypical is the story of a donor representative that had set up an appointment to see an elderly married couple who had once been generous contributors. "On the way over to this couple's house, the husband passed away of a heart attack," Bigham recalled. "Our donor representative showed up an hour after the death. She had previously had a friendly relationship with these people, and when she got to the house, she became a comforter. She prayed and comforted the donor. She helped as they took the body out of the house to the ambulance. She was there to be a part of it."

This was not unusual for people who work for Feed the Children because, Bigham added, "Our job is to be here to serve. We serve not only those who are hungry in Appalachia, the Mississippi delta, and the inner cities. We serve the donors. We are here to be a blessing back to them, to make it possible for them to be blessed in what they're doing. The donor really is king. Ours is as much a ministry to the donor as it is to the barefoot child in the Smoky Mountains. As Larry Jones [founder] says: 'All we are, are the hands and feet of your heart.' "

"We get the blessings of the Lord," concluded Bigham, "but we're consciously trying to do it the Nordstrom way."

THE WAY TO KEEP RELATIONSHIPS SOLID

Relationships are the essence of customer service. If what you are selling is similar to what your competitor is selling, and if your prices are similar to your competitor's prices, how can you get an edge? By developing a strong relationship with your customer—and by never taking that relationship for granted. Customers are looking for people who take responsibility for their actions. Those customers can be very forgiving if they see that you hear the problem and you take care of the problem. Use these reminders to help you build and sustain powerful relationships:

- Measure both feet.
- Seek to understand the customer first.
- Track your sphere of influence.
- Spoil the client whenever possible.
- A referral that comes from a satisfied client is a lot easier to get than new business from a stranger.
- Create a lifetime experience.
- Constantly reinvent yourself.
- Service the client not the project.
- Become a source for new ideas.
- Understand what customers want.
- Take responsibility.
- Thank the customer for the relationship.

5 Empower Employees to Take Ownership

Power flows to the person who knows how.
Responsibilities gravitate to the person who can
shoulder them.

—Elbert Hubbard

If there is a bigger cliché than customer service, it must be empowerment. Think of all the trees that have been sacrificed to print the books written about empowering employees. The fact is: You empower people by giving up the power yourself. If you boil the Nordstrom system down to its essence, down to the one sentence that separates Nordstrom and other great customer service companies from the rest, it is this: Nordstrom gives the people on the sales floor the freedom to make decisions, and management backs them on those decisions. Everything else flows from that simple premise.

Nordstrom is structured like an inverted pyramid (see illustration on page 124). At the very top of the pyramid are the customers, and beneath them are the salespeople, department managers, executives, all the way down to the lowly board of directors. This is both a literal and symbolic way of how the company does its business. The customers are on top because they are

123

Nordstrom's inverted organizational pyramid.

the most important people in the equation. But the next most important are the salespeople because they are the ones who are closest to the customer. And it is the job of the rest of the people in the organization to help those people on the sales floor—the front lines—because they are the engine that powers the machine. If they aren't making money, then the company isn't making money.

In a Nordstrom employee newspaper, salespeople were asked the question: "What does the inverted pyramid mean to me?" Patrice Nagasawa, a top women's wear salesperson answered: "I have direct input on what my customers want and I get an active response from my buying team. What could be better than having your customer tell you what she wants and you get to tell your buyer what the customer told you."

At Realty Executives of Nevada, co-owner Fafie Moore asked her receptionist, Karie Fitzgerald to read *The Nordstrom Way* and then had Karie write out all of her suggestions from the book that would help her better perform in her job. Number one on her list was to get a telephone headset because "It would really free her hands up and she would feel like she was more energized on the phone," recalled Moore. "By that afternoon, everyone in the office had a headset. They were so excited because they had an idea and we acted on that idea right away. It was something so simple, and it wasn't expensive."

Great customer service doesn't have to be the grand gesture; it can be the small gesture, the human kindness. I experienced that at Starbucks Coffee when I visited the store in my neighborhood in West Seattle to buy a pound of Arabian Mocha Java beans. I had with me an empty one-pound bag because when you bring in your empty bag, Starbucks takes 10 cents off the price. I handed my bag to the young woman behind the counter, who looked at it and said, "Your bag is pretty worn out. I'll give you a new bag, but I'll still take 10 cents off the price." I must tell you, that gesture made me feel good. Ten cents off the price. Of course, I paid 13 bucks for the pound of coffee, but the bottom line is that I experienced a positive feeling toward Starbucks.

When I told that story to Howard Schultz, the chairman of Starbucks, he smiled and replied that that is precisely the kind of feeling he wants customers to have—the kind of feeling that Schultz waxes nostalgic about when he recalls his youth:

I remember as a kid, in Brooklyn, I would go to the butcher store with my mom. The butcher would show her the chicken and my mother would say, "No, I don't want that one; yes, I want that one." The butcher placed a lot of importance on doing things right for her. After we were done, he'd always say, "I'll see you next week, Mrs. Schultz." The passion to service and the strong relationship that the local merchant had with the customer have disappeared in America. We are all so hungry to be valued, not only as a customer, but at work, at home, at the post office, whatever it is. So much of our life as a consumer is abusive. We've accepted that because that's what America has become. When you have a nice experience, it's such an anomaly, it's so uplifting and powerful. You want to go into a place—even if it isn't the best place—where you're appreciated, known, and respected.

The only way you can create that kind of place is to empower your employees to think of the customer first. As the people from our featured companies will tell you: It's not easy.

FirstMerit: Put Employees in the Position to Make a Difference

At FirstMerit, the strategic imperative is centered around the theme of "Believing in People," which "keeps us focused on developing and energizing our people," said chairman and CEO John Cochran. "Our goal is to empower the FirstMerit team members—whether a receptionist, a teller, a call center employee, a services division employee, frontline banker or CEO—so that they can serve the customer with a blend of urgency and enthusiasm.

It is a core value at FirstMerit Bank that all employees are continually encouraged to believe that they can make a difference in the life of the customer that they are serving at that moment. In fact, one of the credos at the bank is the phrase, "I make a difference." "We understand that our competitive advantage is in the hands of each individual and only when those hands are part of the team do they provide an unmatched experience for our customers," said Cochran.

As part of employee training, the bank encourages people to take control of any customer situation that they encounter. "We tell them that there's not anything that they can't handle," Cochran emphasized. "This attitude springs from our desire to have a positive impact on our customers through highly energized, empow ered, and focused people, who take ownership of problems, seek new ways to grow, and search for constant improvement."

"Like Nordstrom, we ask our people to use their common sense," Cochran continued. "We want them to ask themselves what action can they take that will fundamentally be best for the customer. It goes back to empowering your people to take ownership of the customer situation. For example, if you have to waive a charge on the spot, you do it. If you have to make an apology for the institution, you do it." Empowerment entails pushing the power down to where it makes a difference with the customer—on the front lines at the 177 First-Merit bank branches. FirstMerit differs from many banks in the fact that there are no managers in its branches. Instead, regional "community bank managers" are each in charge of four branches, but the branches manage themselves.

"The customer's experience in the branch is fully owned by the branch and the employee," said Cochran. "What is absolutely essential is how the branch's employees work together to define and execute the best customer experience at FirstMerit. We say 'every employee is a manager.' So, if the customer says to an employee, 'I want to speak to the manager,' the employee is empowered to tell the customer, 'I can help you.' By doing that, we reinforce the idea to employees that they can make a difference, and it reassures the customer that the situation is in caring hands, and that the right answer will be found, quickly and reliably."

Although empowerment may appear to be a reward to an individual, FirstMerit extends the idea of empowerment to teams. "We understand that our competitive advantage is in the hands of each individual and only when those hands are part of the team do they provide an unmatched experience for our customers," Cochran explained. "We hope that a FirstMerit employee thinks, 'I make a difference to the customer, internally to my team, to the community, and to FirstMerit, but in the end, it is only I who can make the difference happen for all of us.' "

In this team environment, each person recognizes his or her individual contribution to the direction and success of the whole. By sharing trust, purpose, and common goals, FirstMerit people are allowed to take risks and are encouraged to try new initiatives. When an employee lends a hand to solve a problem, or offers a special solution, or pitches in to meet a deadline, the person is singled out through the bank's First Honors recognition program (which will be explained more fully in Chapter 7).

FirstMerit, like many other banks, has been growing through mergers and acquisitions. But this pursuit of greater scale and cost efficiencies often results in more cost-effective centralized decision making, which disempowers the local branches from the communities they serve. FirstMerit is trying to prevent that absence of personal touch by offering service and solutions through empowered branch bankers with the support of centralized operations. The bank believes that finding solutions tailored to the needs of a client is the best formula for maintaining loyalty.

"We believe that local people serving local communities and customers gives us a distinct advantage, because they are the company's eyes and ears in the community," said Cochran. "By keeping all levels of our organization close to the customer, we improve our creativity and responsiveness. We also can learn from each other. By comparing performances among individuals and branches, we discover who does what well, and then we learn from them."

Because empowerment comes with accountability, each FirstMerit branch and department has its own profit-and-loss statement. People at the local level are encouraged to build an entrepreneurial spirit and to create a greater understanding of the direct financial impact they have on FirstMerit's business. By allowing branches to set the pricing on some bank products, FirstMerit believes it can maintain its competitiveness by reacting quickly and efficiently to local changes and demands. Local credit decisions take advantage of the knowledge and judgment of the banker that is nearest to the customer. Regional Vice President George Paidas said that with the corporate focus on decentralization and empowerment, local loan officers are empowered to make decisions and are free to weigh the unique circumstances of a borrower without having to go through hoops with the corporate office.

"We have been empowered to act and to cut much of that stuff," Paidas pointed out. "Loan authority now *means* loan authority. So, if an officer has $100,000 in loan authority and there is a loan with some exceptions, we ask him or her to note those exceptions and gain the approval of our local senior lender. But he doesn't have to go through all kinds of push-ups to get it done. The discussion is in the spirit of assuring us that the exception is well understood and warranted. We've also raised the threshold in terms of what dollar limit on a credit requires that it go to the committee in Akron [where the bank is based]. All in all, we are able to do much more now on a local basis."

USinternetworking: Make Value the Core Service

USinternetworking has empowered its service employees because it is the most effective to way to help clients needing technical assistance. "We knew from the very beginning that we were going to have to serve as a help desk for our clients," said John Tomljanovic, Vice President for Client Care at USi. "A lot of times, when people call in, it's because they're having a problem. It's not because things are going great. We decided we needed to couple account management with relationship building."

Rather than offer the traditional 1–800-HELP call which would connect a client to an anonymous service representative, USi has chosen to personalize the client care function by assigning a dedicated Client Assistance Team (CAT) to each client who has purchased outsourcing services with USi, and assign each client a dedicated 800 number to call for assistance. By directing any and all client contacts to the specific team, USi ensures that the employee who takes the call clearly understands the unique needs of the client and the client's history. Each knowledgeable, highly trained CAT is completely familiar with the technical and functional aspects of the entire USi service portfolio and is empowered to take whatever action is necessary to quickly resolve any client issues. In addition, a team of product-specific application engineers—with expertise in each technology offered by USi—closely supports these front-line teams 24 hours a day, seven days a week.

When USi signs up a new client, the contract includes specific service-level agreements that have to be fulfilled. If USi fails to meet the terms of the service-level agreement, account managers and their CAT teams are empowered to do whatever it takes to satisfy the customer, including issuing a credit [which can run in the tens of thousands of dollars] or giving the client an additional service enhancement at no cost.

"Those decisions don't have to go up through the chain for people to ask me to approve it," Tomljanovic emphasized. "All the account managers and their CAT teams are empowered to make those decisions. If we don't meet an availability uptime of your system, don't pay your bill; we're going to give you a credit for it. Our founder and CEO Chris McCleary tells clients: 'If you're not happy, don't send the payment check in. Don't pay your bill.' "

Tomljanovic recalled that the first time that USi had to give a client a rebate, the vice president of that company called to say it was the first time that any provider have ever done anything like that. "He said it was very nice that we did it, but that he wasn't that interested in the money. I told him, I agreed with him 100 percent. I told him, 'It's not that we can buy you back, but it's a token that we admit that we made a mistake, and we want to fix it and not let it happen again.' The guy has been an advocate for us since that day."

Tomljanovic said it wasn't that difficult to convince account representatives to be comfortable with being empowered because most of the new hires were seasoned veterans—some with 10 to 15 years of experience in similar industries—who understood the importance of taking care of the clients. "At the same time, they're not going to give away the farm. They understand that it's not a good thing to be giving away the company's money, but if we're not doing what we are saying we are going to do, then the client has every right to come back to us and be upset. You have to look at it from a long-term perspective. It's a lot harder to go out and acquire a new client than it is to retain an existing one. If we can keep the clients we have and keep them happy, then we're going to be around for a long time."

The entire company was founded on the idea that you could change the architecture to improve client service. When McCleary started the company in 1998 with one employee, no office, no data center, no bandwidth, and no customers, he asked how the company could eliminate down time and create higher client satisfaction—without regard to costs.

"USi was a company that was developed with a clean slate to accomplish only one mission: to make network applications run better and create higher levels of customer satisfaction," stated McCleary, who eventually raised more than $300 million to finance the company. "That's compared to a lot of telephone companies who are putting in data centers to use up their bandwidth. But the motive is not to improve service to customers but to add bandwidth with value-added services."

Feed the Children: Push the Decision-Making Responsibility and Authority Down to the Lowest Level Possible

Like every great customer-service organization, Feed the Children "wants to push the decision-making responsibility and authority down to the lowest level possible," explained vice president Paul Bigham. "It's a cliché, but we never lose sight of the fact that it is essential to what we do. Our charge to the people who work for Feed the Children is this: 'You can do anything you want as long as you stay within certain parameters. Don't go out of those parameters. Inside those parameters, I don't want to hear from you. If you don't feel comfortable in making the call, go up-line and let someone else make the call.'"

In 1995, when the Alfred P. Murrah Building was bombed by terrorists in Oklahoma City, Feed the Children's hometown, the employees of the charity sprang into action. Director Larry Jones sent out the word to local officials: "If I've got it, you can have it. If I don't have it, I'll find it. If I can't find it, we'll buy it." As Bigham recalled, "That was our mantra for the next few weeks as people worked around the clock."

In the aftermath of the bombing, harried rescue workers spent days removing blocks of concrete, digging through the rubble in a Herculean effort to locate survivors. Those who were there remember it as a surreal scene of debris and destruction, accompanied by the constant humming of generators, which supplied the power to illuminate the building. In the middle of all of that, a sleet storm swept through the scene, adding further misery. Through it all, courageous men and women continued to work in the bitter cold, 12 and 14 hours at a stretch, pulling out dead bodies and parts of dead bodies. When they found they needed metal kneepads to protect them from the shrapnel, Feed the Children located the kneepads, and arranged with American Airlines to fly them into Oklahoma City. "When they took their breaks, the men asked for two things: warm socks and cigars," said Bigham. "Somehow, one of our employees took it upon himself to locate some Tiparillos. I don't remember where we found them, but I delivered them. I'll never forget those guys coming back from this horrid, horrible, grotesque place; this den of death, and just sort of connect to reality again. We wouldn't have been able to do that without a Feed the Children worker empowered to do whatever the job required." In the spring of 1999, a tornado hit Oklahoma City. While Larry Jones took the lead in dealing with media interviews—telling people what was needed and where it was needed and how to get it to Oklahoma City—he empowered a few of his top aides to handle the logistics of the operation.

"We physically took over the street behind us and the parking lot of the companies behind us," recalled Bigham. "They were gracious enough to close down for a day and a half while we brought in 400 truck loads of emergency supplies. The streets were blocked with individuals bringing in everything from bicycles to flashlight batteries to sports drinks and soda pop to baby diapers and baby food." Even more remarkably, when more than 1,500 citizens of the Oklahoma City community came forth to ask how they could help, Feed the Children responded. "We not only empowered our employees, we also empowered volunteers," Bigham added. "We picked volunteers out of the crowd who appeared to have leadership skills. We told them: 'This is your area; you take care of this and you do that.' They would do it. Some drove forklifts, some sorted food. Some of them were so outstanding that we later hired them to work for Feed the Children."

Feed the Children tries to empower everyone who works with them, including the independent service providers who distribute the food to needy organizations. "We try to provide them things that help them do the jobs they are there to do. Feed the Children is not big enough to hand carry a box to every family or hungry child in America," said Bigham. "We need to empower all the people we work with to do what needs to be done."

Mike's Carwash: Make Customers Happy so They Keep Coming Back

"We tell our employees: Do whatever it takes to make a customer happy," emphasized Jerry Dahm, vice president of Mike's. "The guy who started on the job yesterday has just as much authority as a 10-year veteran associate to walk up to a customer and say, 'We're not happy with the wash. We want to give you a rewash. Would you mind going through again?'"

Mike's emphasizes customer satisfaction because the company recognizes the value of a satisfied customer.

"We calculated years ago, not adjusting for inflation or price increases, that the lifetime value of one customer is about $15,000," said Dahm. "So, we really try to teach our people that you can't just look at what the customer is spending today. If you can create happy lifetime customers, who become advocates for our company and refer us to family and friends, you're talking a lot of money. We have many customers in Fort Wayne who have been coming to us for 50 years."

As a vehicle to reward and recognize outstanding customer service by associates, Mike's initiated what the company calls its WOW Program. Every time the company receives a letter or an e-mail praising one of the associates for performing a customer service act above and beyond the call of duty, that associate is given a "WOW" pin, and is rewarded financially, and later with a plaque at the company's annual awards banquet. By emphasizing the WOW experience, and repeatedly telling employees that they are empowered to do whatever it takes to make the customer happy, Mike's has created a culture of empowered employees.

What is a WOW moment and how can you employ it? It could be something as simple as fixing the flat tire of a noncustomer who was stranded near a Mike's Carwash or driving home a customer who accidentally locked his keys in his car. And it could be something as dramatic as saving a choking child by performing the Heimlich maneuver. For your business, it could be a host of other opportunities for customer service.

Great customer service companies give their people the power to make the situation right—right away. One Friday afternoon, an elderly couple brought their car in to Mike's before leaving town to visit their son in Michigan. They bought "The Works"—Mike's ultimate service of washing and shining—in preparation for the special weekend. After taking their car through the wash, the couple came back around and parked in the front of Mike's building. When they got out of their car, manager Monte Montgomery who came up to greet them, saw immediately that the woman was obviously upset. She told him that while sitting in her car as it went through the automated wash, the high pressure rinse was too strong, water squirted through her window, and she had gotten her hair wet. To make matters worse, she had just come from the beauty parlor where she had just gotten a perm for the big weekend. "From what I could tell, the couple's car had a bad seal around their window or maybe it was down just a bit," recalled Montgomery. "She, of course, saw it otherwise. I apologized and asked how I could resolve this. She said, 'I want you to fix my hair!'"

Suddenly terrified, Montgomery asked her if she meant that he specifically had to do her hair. No, she said, she preferred to return to the beauty parlor. The woman and her husband left to have lunch at a fast-food restaurant next door. Montgomery found them there, apologized for what had happened and refunded their money. Not only that, "I told her to have her hair done again and that would be on Mike's, too," said Montgomery. "They greatly appreciated this and continued to be regular customers at Mike's."

Concepts Worldwide: Don't Attach a Dollar Value to Good Judgment

Terri Breining, the founder and CEO of Concepts Worldwide told me that the best way to ensure empowered employees is to first "lavish trust" on them. "Trust is a gift; its bounds have no limits when given openly without reservation or condition. To receive trust, you must extend it first," she said. Breining subscribed to the Nordstrom approach of encouraging empowered employees to use their good judgment.

"We don't attach a dollar value to good judgment," she explained. "We tell our associates: 'You are a professional. We count on your good judgment.' We don't present them with a set of rules and some options. We believe that everything is optional—how they behave; the decisions they make; the recommendations they make. We constantly reinforce good judgment." But, invariably, empowered people are going to use poor judgment. What happens then?

"I tell our people from the time they come to work at Concepts, that no one will ever be fired for making a mistake," said Breining. "If they make the same mistake several times, then we'll have another discussion. If you make a mistake and learn from it, then we're not going to have a problem. When they use poor judgment, we tell them so, and ask them how they would do something differently the next time. We walk through the situation with them and help them think through the process, so it becomes a learning opportunity."

If the associate is unsure as to what to do next, Breining makes sure that a representative of senior management is available for a reality check. A senior manager will make a suggestion about taking care of the client, and will ask the employee what he thinks should be done. "Then, we'll kick it around, and decide on the best direction to take. We never say, 'That's a stupid idea.' We always give them another option. Then I back that up with action. We don't throw tantrums or yell. People are treated like responsible adults and, not surprisingly, they respond by acting like responsible adults." At Concepts Worldwide, they not only accept that employees will use good judgment—they expect that and are counting on it.

"We still need to be profitable; we expect our project managers [who make their own judgments on how many people to staff on site] to make sure that their projects are brought in within budget, and that the clients are happy," Breining pointed out. "Within those parameters, they are relatively free to do whatever they have to do as long as it's not illegal or immoral. The contracts we have with clients spell out what we will do for them. That's the guideline, but project managers can do it whatever way they want. Each of our meeting planners has a different style of doing those things."

Breining offered some examples for the kind of empowered, on-the-spot judgments that some of her employees have had to make. "Once, a client was about to be sent an invoice that included charges for an on-site visit by one of our staff members who was no longer with the company. The planner who worked on that event decided to deduct the charges as an act of good faith, in order to preserve the good client relationship," Breining recalled. "When on-site at an event, employees are empowered to use their best judgment in handling special VIP's or customer satisfaction challenges by ordering gifts or services to please or appease the attendees."

At another meeting, a client resisted help from the Concepts Worldwide planner. The client insisted that, in order to ensure consistency, he would take care of some of the functions that Concepts normally handles. "We allowed this, with some reservations," Breining admitted. "Although all throughout the planning process we experienced difficulties with the client, we did our best to satisfy his needs. At the same time, we still adhered to the policies we absolutely needed in order to ensure the success of the meeting. As it turned out, everything went smoothly and the attendees were happy, and the client later sent us a note thanking us for a successful meeting."

Sometimes, a good employer can empower an associate to grow and flourish simply by just being open. "Due to the company belief of supporting and encouraging staff to share their views, no matter how opposing they may be, I am learning to be assertive and to have confidence in my opinions," said Sommer Tiffany, a young employee at Concepts.

> *During my second week here, I had an uncomfortable discussion with one of the directors. I was encouraged to go to that director and let her know how uncomfortable she made me feel. Trembling and incredibly nervous, I went into the office expecting a confrontation. To my utter amazement, the director thanked me for bringing it to her attention and congratulated me for my courage. I couldn't believe it! If we find an area in which we excel or have an interest in and wish to do more of, we are given the support of the company. This allows people to shift into roles that work best for them, which in turn provides Concepts with a better employee. I have never heard anyone say, "You can't do that here." We are given the responsibility of making that decision for ourselves.*

W Hotel: Hire People Who Are Not Afraid of Taking Ownership

In December 1999, when downtown Seattle was in chaos because of the rioting of protesters who tried to disrupt the meeting of the World Trade Association, there was at least one offbeat love story amidst the pandemonium. James Swift and Lucky Taylor had met in Paris at a chocolate factory, fell in love, and quickly decided to move to Seattle and get married. While staying at the W, Ms. Taylor stopped by the desk of cast member Dan Petzoldt to tell him that she was getting married.

"I asked her where she was going to have the ceremony and she said, 'That's one of the things I want to talk with you about,' " recalled Petzoldt. "She said that she wanted to be near the water. I asked her when she was getting married and she said 'tomorrow.' She and Mr. Swift had decided to elope and get married during this exciting time in Seattle." Petzoldt was able to arrange for the ceremony and reception at Salty's restaurant in West Seattle, which has a spectacular view of downtown Seattle. "As an afterthought, I asked her if there was anything else she would need," said Petzoldt. "She said, 'Yes. I need a photographer, flowers, and an appointment to get my hair done.' " As she listed all her needs, Petzoldt felt his eyes "getting bigger and bigger. But she was very calm about the whole thing. She knew it was unique and she was enjoying it, too."

Petzoldt asked Ms. Taylor if she had secured a minister, and indeed she had. But the minister called her a couple of hours earlier and told her that he was going to be participating in an anti-WTO demonstration and didn't know if he'd be done protesting in time to make the ceremony. "We laughed about that," said Petzoldt. "As I turned to my computer to start searching for churches, Ms. Taylor told me that she had heard of a Web site where you can go online and become an ordained minister over a period of time. I laughed. I thought it was a joke. But when she asked if I'd be willing to do that, I said I would."

At this point, Petzoldt had arranged everything else, so the minister was the last hurdle. He logged on to the Web site and filled out the application; the following day, he received his authorization. To add an additional challenge for Petzoldt, because the couple had met in Paris, when they wrote their own vows, a portion was in French. So Petzoldt had to be tutored in French pronunciation. Nevertheless, right on schedule, he married the couple, far away from the protesters and tear gas. He did all this with the backing of hotel manager Tom Limberg, who cheered on his empowered employee.

In every room at every W Hotel, there is a telephone key marked "Whatever/Whenever." When a guest presses that key, an empowered employee is at the ready to fulfill virtually any (legal) request. "We tell cast members [the term for W employees] if you fail to get a guest whatever they want whenever they want it, then you've failed," said Guy Hensley, vice president of W Hotels. "We don't want you to have to go to a manager. Do whatever you have to do to get whatever you need to make the guest happy. The manager is not going to be able to help them satisfy the guest; they should be able to do it themselves."

When a guest presses the "Whatever/Whenever" key in the room, there's no telling what the request might be. One time, a reporter asked an employee at the W New York to locate a burial plot for his dog, which he claimed had just died. W found a pet cemetery on Long Island. On another occasion, a guest asked for enough chocolate to melt and fill a bathtub. W charged the guest for the cost of the chocolate but not for the expense associated with securing the chocolate, melting it, and getting it into the tub. Thomas Martin, Casting Director for W believed, "One of the biggest pitfalls of empowerment is telling people they are empowered, but also realizing that there are boundaries to that empowerment. It makes them nervous if they go too far." Martin felt that W has helped combat that nervousness by creating a friendly, unthreatening environment between cast members and their managers, "So when they know that their ultimate goal is to please this guest or to correct that situation, they feel comfortable doing it because the end result is what we want: guest satisfaction."

Limberg, the manager of W Seattle, admitted that, on the one hand, he disliked the word "empowerment" because it's a cliché. On the other hand, he said, "It is a beautiful word because it's exactly what you want. You want it embodied in your building. Empowerment is an environment without rules or guidelines. A lot of people are comfortable only with black and white. Our business is gray. We tell this to our people in organization: If you need black and white, go now. It's okay. You won't be happy here. You have to hire the people who are not afraid of taking ownership."

On the very first day that W Seattle opened in 1999, one of the bellmen (called a Welcome Ambassador in W parlance) came to Limberg and asked, point blank: "So, how far are we going to go with this Whatever/Whenever thing?" Limberg saw that the bellman was testing the waters. Where, he wanted to know, was the commitment?

"I said, 'Jackson: What do we need?'" recalled Limberg. "He said, the guests up in this room requested a CD that's not on our list. I asked him what they requested. It was 'Billy Joel's Greatest Hits.' I asked him where he thought we could get it. He said Borders down the street. I said, 'Let's get some petty cash and get it.' Jackson got his question answered. The customer knew darn well that we didn't have it on the list, but we made it happen. At the end of the day, I've got another great CD on the list; turns out it was a double CD. This was not an expenditure; it was an investment. You invest in your future by taking the proper care of your customers and the people you work with—in equal shares."

St. Charles Medical Center:
Back Up Your Employees

When the W Hotel employee asked Tom Limberg how far the company was willing to go with this idea of empowerment, it illustrated that it takes more than just talk to make employees feel that management is backing them up. St. Charles Medical Center faced the same challenge. In fact, because St. Charles was already an established institution, empowerment was an even tougher sell. When Jim Lussier was promoted from president to chief executive officer of St. Charles in 1989, the hospital had little competition in the Bend, Oregon, area, and its operating margins surpassed the average in the industry. Lussier's primary goal was to maintain St. Charles's operational competency while adding the customer-service focus of Nordstrom.

At a time when managed care was about to dominate the health care industry and consumers were increasingly unhappy about higher costs, Lussier felt that the system had to become more responsive to the needs of the patients by empowering employees to give great customer service. Lussier believed employees simply had to become more involved than ever, rather than depend on a thick layer of middle management, which placed too much power in the hands of too few people and created an "us vs. them" relationship between middle managers and frontline employees, a situation that stifled innovation.

Lussier and other colleagues, who shared his vision, knew that the road to customer service would be accomplished by giving a voice to the employees on the frontline of patient care. Lussier intended to dramatically reconstruct St. Charles's organizational chart by reducing it to three tiers: executive, leadership, and operations, with the leadership tier (many of the executives within it were former department heads), as much accountable to employees as they were to executives. But when patient-centered care programs were put in place, seemingly to the satisfaction of employees, the lack of results was baffling. "We pushed the launch button," Lussier recalled. "And nothing happened."

The problem was that employees were not buying into the top-down reorganization because management neglected to gather the input from the frontline people who were, theoretically, the beneficiaries of the new policy. When they were surveyed in private, workers voiced a myriad of fears and concerns because they felt that "restructuring" was another word for widespread layoffs. In addition, they didn't believe management's doctrine of total honesty; in fact, they were less inclined to believe management. Showing that it didn't lack a sense of humor, the management group placed a book of meeting minutes near the employee entrance and wryly entitled it "Really Secret Stuff You're Not Supposed to Know."

Objections were expressed at town-meeting-like hospital forums where employees grew increasingly brave when they saw that they wouldn't be punished. Middle managers, who were about to lose both status and authority, didn't have much to say. A frustrated Lussier told those managers, "The train's leaving the station. Get on with all your heart and support or get off." Not surprisingly, several managers left for other positions. For those who stayed, Lussier offered this olive branch: "If this restructuring does not achieve what we expect and it affects quality, we will stop the experiment."

To implement employee empowerment, St. Charles had to first completely change its entire organizational approach—not an easy thing to do in the hierarchical world of health care, where the physician was king. In 1989, the hospital went from 55 operating departments to 16 clusters formed around common duties. Out of those clusters came empowered, self-directed work teams who were in charge of conducting daily operations.

"That was important in terms of sending out the message that (1) the future is going to be different from the past, and (2) the individuals and the team have the decision-making capabilities for handling patient and staff problems," recalled Lussier. "It was really difficult to do that in a health care environment because you couldn't tell a nurse that she has a right to change a physician's order for a drug prescription for a patient. Nurses took those kinds of strict edicts and applied them to everything. They would say to a patient, 'I know you didn't get your food at 1 o'clock, but there's nothing I can do about that,' when in fact there's everything that they can do about that, as well as a lot of the other problems or issues that surround patients and families."

By working in clusters, employees could more easily talk to each other, so the time spent on chart documentation was cut by 50 percent in the first year. Also, the presurgery clinic produced the most sensational results: zero scheduling delays, zero lost orders. Waiting times, which previously reached as much as eight hours were reduced to an average of an hour and a half. For employees, the most important result is that massive layoffs never occurred; the staff decreased through attrition by 10 percent.

Lussier felt that the only way to make people feel comfortable about being empowered was for St. Charles to establish training programs that emphasized the point that people-centered teams have the power to accomplish important tasks on their own.

Eventually, Lussier and his management team began to see results. As workers began to accept the new, empowering way of doing business, they began offering creative ideas to promote better customer service, including: 24-hour room service, which enabled patients and staff to order food at any time; replacing pagers with cell phones so that nurses could respond more quickly to calls; and placing minipharmacies on several hospital floors rather than just one in the basement. They stopped making it mandatory for patients to check into the presurgery clinic by 6 AM. "That early check-in wasn't necessary for patients," Lussier says, "but it sure was convenient for us."

Suddenly, employees started taking this empowerment idea seriously. For example, in the midst of a national shortage of a particular blood medication, Bertie Perone, a veteran nurse, was told there was no way she could get any more of the medication. Taking the initiative, on her own shift, she called the president of the pharmaceutical company that made the medication, and three days later she secured a two-month supply.

"That was amazing to me," said Lussier. "Five years ago, she wouldn't have thought that she had the capability to do that. Those kinds of symbols really empower the rest of the staff." Lussier and his staff were able to

pull out of this change because they had the backing of the hospital board as well as Sister Catherine
Hellmann, the former chief executive officer, who was
something of a policy-tweaker herself. (She once looked
the other way when a young boy smuggled in a puppy to
give to his grandfather, who was a patient at the hospital. Years later, that young puppy-smuggler reintroduced
himself to Sister Catherine at a medical conference; he
had been inspired to go to medical school and become a
doctor.)

Perhaps St. Charles's finest flourish in its empowerment program was to help all employees think of themselves—and call themselves—caregivers. "The idea is
that everybody is here to be a caregiver, whether it's a
chief executive officer or a registered nurse on the PM
shift. Everybody can do that," Lussier stated categorically. "So, when you're in a patient's room and you notice that they don't have any water, it's not the registered
nurse's job to get the water. You are able to take care of
that need. We train people in doing that. They are aware
they can perform routine sorts of things. It isn't skill-
specific; it's about customer service."

Finally, Lussier has this advice for other companies
and organizations: "The business that is not maximiz-
ing the use of its workforce is a business that's doomed
to failure."

Continental Airlines:
Trust People to Do a Good Job

In early 1995, Continental Airlines made a conscious
decision to empower its employees. "We have guidelines
that cover the way we want to handle whatever situations we can envision arising. But we tell our people

that when something comes up that's not covered in the guidelines, we want them to make the decision that is not only good for the customer, but also good for the company. We're not interested in giving the customer everything he wants. We want the balance and will support whatever our employees come up with," said chairman and CEO Gordon Bethune.

When Bethune was hired in late 1994 to turn around the carrier, the only way he could bring in the best people to help a failing company was to empower them. "I had to give 100 percent autonomy to the guy in charge of pricing," he recalled. "He didn't have to clear it with me. He wanted to do that because he had never worked in an environment where he could call the shots. He would come to work here believing we were going to get the place fixed, but he wanted to come to work in an environment where he had autonomy. That's a huge attraction. When you have a say regarding how things operate around here, that's when you begin to buy into the team. We had to change a lot of middle management to get them to do it that way."

Do these empowered people make mistakes? Sure. "If you make a huge mistake, we will show you the way we'd have preferred that you handle it. You're not going to get in trouble for it," said Bethune, but "if you consistently can't make a good decision, we'll probably have to take you out of the decision-making process. But if a pilot landed long and went off the end of the runway into the mud, we're not going to make him a plumber."

Bethune has found that, "Knowing you can say what you want makes for a day-and-night difference in how our people do their jobs. They know that nobody is going to second guess everything that they do. You just have to trust the people to do a good job."

THE WAY TO EMPOWER EMPLOYEES

Regardless of the kind of business you are in, empowerment is always possible. In fact, it's not only possible, it's necessary. Good employees will need to have autonomy and have their decisions respected. They don't just want to push papers or give rote answers; they want to have an impact on the future of the organization. Here's how great customer-service companies empower their people:

- Trust the people you hire.
- Hire people who are looking to assume responsibility and ownership.
- Give them the freedom to make decisions on the spot.
- Teach employees that with empowerment comes accountability.
- Push the decision-making responsibility and authority down to the lowest level possible.
- Encourage employees every step of the way.
- When empowered people use poor judgment, use those mistakes as tools for learning.
- Don't attach a dollar value to good judgment.
- Make value a core service.
- Commit 100 percent to empowerment.

Disregard the Rules and Be Innovative

*It is not enough that you form, and even follow,
the most excellent rules for conducting yourself
in the world; you must, also, know when to
deviate from them, and where lies the exception.*
—Lord Greville

You've just been hired at Nordstrom. But before you set foot on the sales floor, you must first go through employee orientation, which includes a day-long session that focuses almost exclusively on customer service. You're seated at a table in the training room, and in front of you is placed a grey 5″ x 7″ card, entitled "Nordstrom Rule Book," which contains the words in the box on page 152.

That's it. One rule. Use your good judgment in all situations. For some people, this corporate philosophy is thrilling! It's liberating! "My manager is not only respecting my opinions, she's going to let me exercise my judgment." For others, being given just a single rule is terrifying.

In the early 1990s, when Nordstrom was hiring for a new store in the Washington, DC, suburb of Pentagon City, Virginia, the company received many job

WELCOME TO NORDSTROM

We're glad to have you with our Company.

Our number one goal is to provide outstanding customer service.

Set both your personal and profession goals high.

We have great confidence in your ability to achieve them.

Nordstrom Rules:

Rule #1: Use your good judgment in all situations.

There will be no additional rules.

Please feel free to ask your department manager, store manager, or division general manager any question at any time.

applications from individuals who had worked in the military and federal bureaucracies. One former bureaucrat actually told a Nordstrom executive, "If you give me a hundred rules, I'll be the best darn employee you ever had. But one rule? I don't think so." That kind of person doesn't want freedom; he wants to be told what to do. Unless you are looking for an automaton don't hire that person. "Because we don't have too many rules, we don't have to worry if we're breaking them," Annette Carmony, a Nordstrom employee in the Salem, Oregon store told me. "We're judged on our performance, not our obedience to orders."

James F. Nordstrom, the beloved co-chairman, who passed away in 1996, hated rules because they got in the way of customer service and the Nordstrom philosophy of empowering employees. Jim felt that the more rules an organization has, the farther and farther the organization moves away from its customers. When that happens, the rules become the most important consideration to employees; not the customer. It's as if these unempowered employees wrap the rules around them like a security blanket, and then proclaim to the customer: "You can't hurt me. I'm protected by the rules."

Jim Nordstrom once explained to me, "The minute you come up with a rule you give an employee a reason to say 'no' to a customer. That's the reason we hate rules. We don't want to give an employee a reason—from us [management]—to say 'no' to a customer. We feel that the majority of the people we hire want to do a good job and want to be successful. I think that's true of most companies." Jim felt that after people are hired, management at many companies does "vicious things" that turn off employees and take the fun out of people's jobs. "If you give them a hundred rules, you've taken away any empowerment that they can have."

Back in the days when Jim and his brother John and cousin Bruce ran the company (from the late 1960s through the mid-1990s), Jim was fiercely protective of Nordstrom's freewheeling entrepreneurial culture and was willing to fight to do whatever it took to maintain it—even if it meant challenging employee grievances over wrongful termination. He once declared, "I would rather we lost lawsuits from time to time than keep employees who are not up to our standards. Because a weak employee will make the others around him weak, and drag them down." With that in mind, the company tore up its rule book and told its managers, in Jim Nordstrom's words: "You can't rely on these rules. You can't sit back and wait for an employee to break a rule and then get rid of them. You have to sit down with them, one on one, and communicate."

Kathleen Lee-Geist was a 42-year-old resident of Friday Harbor, a little town on San Juan Island, which is a part of the San Juan Islands in Washington State. On a Friday in early summer 1998, Lee-Geist was returning home from Seattle after having endured three difficult days of treatment for a brain tumor at the Virginia Mason Medical Center. She was resting, nearly immobilized, in the back of her van, which her husband David was driving, as they waited at the dock at Anacortes to catch the car ferry back to Friday Harbor. On summer days, particularly Fridays, ferryboats are often late, lines are long, and tempers are short.

Lee-Geist was dying and she wanted desperately to spend her final hours at home. Anticipating that the woman faced a long wait on the ferry dock, her doctor had given her a letter that instructed ferry workers to give her "priority-loading" status, which would get her on the next departing boat. But when David Lee-Geist presented the letter, the ferry worker told him that they would not be boarding the next boat because they had violated the rules. According to the code of the Washington State Transportation Commission, the letter should have been *faxed* 24 hours ahead of time. Because this had not been done, in the eyes of the ferry system, the Lee-Geists' situation did not qualify as an emergency. Therefore, they would have to wait their turn, which would mean several hours, at least.

David Lee-Geist pleaded their case to a series of ferry workers and officials, but each and every one turned him down with the same basic answer: "the rules." Frustrated to the point of tears, he asked to speak to a supervisor. But the number he was given turned out to be a recording. By the time he got a phone number that worked, the supervisor was not accessible because it was after 5 PM.

A friend of the Lee-Geists, who was herself returning from the hospital and had already been granted a medical-priority loading, also implored four ferry workers to let Kathy on the boat. But the workers adamantly refused, again citing the fact that the Lee-Geists "didn't follow the procedure." When the ferry finally arrived, the friend, who was in pain herself, told the ferry workers that she would relinquish her place in line so that the Lee-Geists could board the boat. A worker told her that if she didn't get on the ferry, neither she nor the Lee-Geists would get on. The disconsolate woman boarded the ferry.

Meanwhile, the Lee-Geists waited in line for an additional 2½ hours. By the time they made it home, it was five hours after they first arrived at the dock at Anacortes. Kathleen Lee-Geist passed away the next night. At her memorial service, her friend, the author Tom Robbins, read a piece he wrote specifically for a woman who had been extremely popular and respected in her community. So, what happened? Why couldn't a dying woman get home?

Turns out, for the three months prior to the Lee-Geist episode, the ferry staff had been following a new procedure manual—*12 volumes worth*. According to regulations spelled out in that manual, a pig heading for a 4-H meeting would have had higher priority for boarding than a woman dying of a brain tumor.

"I'm afraid the Lee-Geist family didn't fit the Washington Administrative Code and didn't fit our instructions," conceded Joseph Nortz, the director of marine operations for the Washington State Ferries. The agent was faced with a choice, Nortz claimed: "Do I make an exception or do I follow these instructions?" Obviously, for the agent, the decision was simple: Follow instructions. Employees of the ferry system told the Seattle newspapers that the Lee-Geist episode was unavoidable because the top-down system in which they work rewards employees who adhere to the rules and don't use their own good judgment.

A spokeswoman defended the ferry workers because they have to be on the lookout for people who try to cheat the system by feigning illness. "We get letters from doctors on cocktail napkins telling us to give priority loading to someone," said the spokeswoman. She cited an instance when an apparently pregnant woman hurriedly arrived at the dock and announced that she was in labor and had to board immediately. As workers rushed her onto the vessel, the pillow she was hiding under her shirt slipped out and fell to the ground.

"What you saw in Anacortes is that the dock person was trapped," a veteran employee told the *Seattle Times*. "If he would have violated the written rules, and anybody had phoned [to complain], he or she would have been beached. They're getting rules so that people don't have room to have compassion." The ferry system responded to the Lee-Geist story with yet a new set of rules that would enable people with valid medical conditions or other emergency situations to be moved to the front of the line. A motorist with a doctor's note stipulating that a prolonged delay would cause "detrimental health risks" to an occupant of the vehicle will be permitted to get on the next available boat. The new policy stated that priority loading could be granted to someone without a doctor's note, depending on the best judgment of the frontline employees.

A spokeswoman for Washington State Ferries apologized for the incident, said that it shouldn't have happened, and that the supervisor who made the decision "feels terrible," and defended the unnamed employee as "the kind of guy who goes by the rules. He's a great employee, but he made a mistake in this instance. Sometimes, when you see a situation like this, you have to make the judgment from your heart."

Have you ever been faced with a situation in your company where you knew that you had to make a judgment from your heart? And did you feel empowered enough to make that judgment—right or wrong?

Nordstrom has a 100-percent money-back guarantee on virtually all of its merchandise (cosmetics represent an exception, for health reasons). Do people abuse that guarantee? You bet they do. After all is said and done, what percentage of the population is dishonest? Nordstrom has taken a stand that it does not want to penalize the 98 percent of the people in the world who are honest because of the actions of the 2 percent of people who are dishonest.

Does your company have that attitude? Or do you assume that 98 percent of your customers are dishonest, so you use your rules as protection against those customers?

But we, as customers, don't care what your rules are. And while we're at it, we don't much care about the process, the bureaucracy, or the system either. We only want someone to take care of us. One summer not long ago, my wife and I flew to Los Angeles, where I had some business. After renting a car at the Los Angeles airport, we spent a couple of days in Los Angeles, and then we drove south to Orange County for a little rest and relaxation at the beautiful Ritz-Carlton Hotel in Laguna

Niguel. One night, we were driving around Laguna Beach and the icon for the engine lights up on the dashboard. I don't know very much about cars, but I figure that this is not a good thing, so I consulted the owner's manual, which said that if the engine icon lights up, you should contact your dealer immediately. The following morning, I called the rental car agency and told them of the problem. The young man who answered the phone said, "Fine, drive the car back up to John Wayne Airport [a 45-minute drive up the freeway] and we'll give you a new car."

What? "First of all," I tell the young man, "I'm on vacation. Second of all, we know there is something wrong with the engine of this car, and you want me to drive 45 minutes up the freeway. No, I want you to bring me a new car to my hotel."

His answer: "We can't do that. There's a rule against that."

Undaunted, I ask to speak to his supervisor. She eventually gets on the phone and I explain the situation to her. And guess what? She doesn't want to bring me a new car either.

At this point, I'm forced to bring out The Big Gun, the nuclear weapon I save for situations just like this. "Look," I tell the supervisor, "I wrote this book on customer service. I speak to business groups all over the country about good customer service and bad customer service. And if you don't bring me a new car, in my next speech, I'm going to cite your company as an example of terrible service." Please feel free to use this line because it gets results.

Forty-five minutes later, a new car arrives at the hotel. A friendly representative of the rental car agency hands me the keys to the new car, I give him the keys to the old car, and he drives off into the sunset. So, obviously, it could be done. But it was much easier for this company to give their employees lots of rules and no discretion.

What kind of rules do you place in front of your employees? If you're an employee, what kind of company rules do you absolutely despise? Take the time to go through all your rules as if you've never seen them before. Evaluate each rule on its own merits. Was a rule instituted several years ago for some forgotten reason that no longer applies today? If that's the case, GET RID OF IT!

The companies that are emulating customer service the Nordstrom Way are constantly simplifying the rules that govern how the companies are run. Richard Kessler of Kessler's Diamond Center in Milwaukee, tells his employees to "Make decisions based on the values that we all agree that you believe in. If you make a decision based on those values, you're doing the right thing." Kessler's Diamond Center's simple mission statement reads: We are dedicated and committed to totally satisfying the needs of our clients based on integrity. "If you follow our mission statement," said Kessler, "you can't make a wrong decision."

At Realty Executives of Nevada, "We try to not have too many rules, and try not to have negative rules," stated co-owner and president Fafic Moore. "I'm always telling people who work for me: 'If you can find a better way to do something, please come tell me about it. If we can eliminate something that we are doing so that it gives us more time to do something else that is more valuable in helping the customer, please tell me about it. If you go home and tell your husband or wife, "If I owned that company, this is what I would do," I want you to tell me that.' That's how I get my most valuable ideas."

John Tomljanovic, Vice President of Client Care at USinternetworking in Annapolis, Maryland, said his company's number one rule is, "The clients must be satisfied. Everything is tied to the clients' satisfaction. If they are not satisfied, then we are not doing the job we said we would do. We broke all the rules in the way we put together the entire customer service component of our organization. We didn't view customer service as a necessary evil. We saw customer service as a key differentiator as a company. The client is the number one priority on everyone's mind in client care."

Continental Airlines: Do What's Right for the Customer and Right for the Company

When Gordon Bethune took over as CEO of Continental Airlines in 1994, he was faced with a dispirited, mistrusting organization that had gone through a series of failed management regimes. Bethune knew that employee manuals were just a storehouse of regulations that were often created for specific circumstances, but somehow eventually "spread far beyond their applicability and become calcified into dumb rote," Bethune wrote in his book, *From Worst to First.*

The Continental employee manual was a compilation of maddeningly specific rules and regulations that ranged from the shade of pencil that had to be used to mark boarding passes to the type of meals that could be served to delayed passengers. To make matters worse, the manual so specifically described job responsibilities that employees were unable to deviate from them for fear of grave punishment. The gate agent was forbidden from clearing up problems. The previous management had preferred that agents just stand there and feel the wrath of frustrated passengers. "Well, nobody likes to work like that. Nobody likes to be treated like a robot, like a little kid who can't solve a problem and make a contribution," wrote Bethune.

To dramatically make the point that things were going to be different from now on, Bethune needed to come up with a sensational symbol of changing times. So, one day, he assembled a number of employees, gave them copies of the manual, and led them on a parade out to the parking lot. There, the employees summarily set the manuals on fire, a task they thoroughly enjoyed. "And we sent word into the field that henceforth we wanted our employees to use their judgment, not follow some rigid manual," wrote Bethune. From that moment on, Continental employees were told that when they had to deal with a situation that was not addressed in their training, they were to follow one simple rule: "Do what was right for the customer and right for the company." Is that a conflicting message? No, just a more nuanced one. Bethune wanted employees who would neither blindly do everything for the customer without worry about expense, nor merely follow procedures that would alienate the customers. He wanted employees to consider both the interests of the customer and the interests of the company. The best way to deal with uncomfortable situations was to use good judgment.

Those of you who fly a lot are well aware of the controversy over the number and size of carry-on bags. Many airlines are clamping down on the carry-on rules, which contrarian Continental is challenging. Continental took a stand against making their customers have to submit to putting their bags in the "sizer" that's usually posted at the security checkpoints. "All those kinds of rules for bags just insulate the employees from the customer," Bethune told me. Hiding behind the rules, employees "don't have to take any indictment for their lack of customer service. So I tell our flight attendants, 'If you can find room for that guy's bag, let's find it. The flight attendants can do whatever they want as long as they meet the federal air regulations.'"

After the manuals were literally and symbolically burned, Continental formed a task force of employees to evaluate every rule and regulation. As a result, they were replaced with more general guidelines for direction, rather than a rule for every inevitability, because Bethune knew that the original rules would destroy the creativity of employees. "We started teaching the deployment of the guidelines; that's when it had the real meaningful effect," said Bethune, who said that the whole process was a learning experience for management. "If you make employees do the right thing, then they will. Our whole customer service emphasis has been first on treating our employees like they deserve everything we can do for them to do their job well, which includes letting them have some autonomy on how it's done." Looking back on that bonfire in the parking lot, Bethune told me he was of the opinion that, "Every company probably ought to burn their employee manual every now and then."

Mike's Carwash: Follow Only One Golden Rule

Mike's Carwash has the right idea. The company has boiled its set of rules down to the Big One: The Golden Rule. "We don't try to wear our associates down with a lot of rules. Everybody knows how they like to be treated when and where they spend their money," explained Bill Dahm, president of Mike's. "My dad [who started the company] said that whenever we make a decision, we ask ourselves: 'How it will affect the customer? If I was in the customer's shoes, how would I feel?' We learned a long time ago that we're selling a service, and if we can do the service really fast, they'll come back and often."

An appreciation of the Golden Rule is an essential aspect of employee training. "One way to really drive home to associates the kind of behavior we're looking for is to ask them to relate to how they feel when they go to a music store to buy a CD or go to Nordstrom to buy some clothes," said Dahm. "In our training, we spend a lot of time discussing experiences that our associates have had in other businesses. We talk about experiences that made them feel good, where they felt appreciated and they got their money's worth. We also talk with them about the kinds of places they've shopped where the salespeople treated them as if they were in the way. For example, one of our pet peeves is going to a store—a place where you want to spend your money—and the salesperson is talking to someone on the phone. You're a paying customer, right there on the property, yet the person on the phone is getting all the attention."

Mike's, like Nordstrom, does have a handbook that serves as a guide to things like benefits, as well as policies prohibiting stealing, smoking on the property, and so on, but when it comes to customer service, Mike's, again like Nordstrom, likes to keep it simple.

"The biggest thing we tell associates to do is to exceed customers' expectations without slowing the operation down," Dahm stressed. "When someone gets his car egged, that stuff does not come off with a carwash. You have to use some compound and some wax to remove it. It wouldn't be uncommon for one of my associates to say to the customer, 'We're not too busy. Pull your car over here and let me clean it off for you.' "

But that is more complicated than it sounds because Mike's is an operation that is built on speed. During the cleaning process, the customers stay in the car, which is run through a tunnel where the car is cleaned, dried (without toweling), and shined.

"The typical carwash has what I call 'task interference,'" described Dahm. "People come up with all these things that customers want. But sometimes, in your desire to please customers and do everything they want, it slows things down. If you get an operation like ours running too slow, people will choose not to come as often because we live in a society where people's time is the currency."

Although Mike's does not offer interior cleaning, the company does provide places on the property where customers can buy time to use high-suction vacuum cleaners and do the job themselves. Vending machines provide supplies to clean windows, dashboards, and so on. Despite all these on-site facilities, an eager, but inexperienced young employee, "once got carried away," Dahm recalled. "When someone came in and wanted the inside cleaned, instead of saying, 'I'm sorry. We don't do that. We have a facility here for you.' He would say, 'Let me help you,' and do it for them. No charge. The problem was that when he was cleaning the customer's car, nobody was doing his job. We had to remind him what he could do and what he couldn't do for the customer." Again, it all comes back to basic judgment.

Concepts Worldwide: Eliminate—or Minimize— Employee Handbooks

For years, Terri Breining, founder and president of Concepts Worldwide, the meeting planning company, resisted putting together an employee handbook, "because I hate them," she said. "But I finally was convinced that we needed something that talked about work days, holidays, and so on. But we don't have anything written down that talks about how to deal with customers. Like Nordstrom, we not only accept that employees will use good judgment, but we are expecting that and we're counting on that."

The contracts that Concepts enters into with clients spell out the guidelines of exactly what the firm will do for the customer on a particular project. But beyond the basic guideline, project managers are unencumbered with a lot of rules and are allowed "to do the job whatever way they want to," explained Breining. "Each of our meeting planners has a different style of doing those things." Because of the individual styles of the project managers, sometimes clients can choose the manager they want to work with. "We've had experiences where a client and one of our meeting planners didn't get along. We don't have a rule that the client has to work with that particular planner."

Obviously, Concepts Worldwide, like every other business, needs to be profitable, and "We expect our project managers to make sure that their projects are brought in within budget, and that the clients are happy," said Breining. "But within those parameters, they are relatively free to do whatever they have to do—as long as it's not illegal or immoral."

For example, Concepts Worldwide managers frequently are required to make on-site judgments about staffing. "If we come up against a situation where it looks like a project is looking like it's going to cost us more than we planned, then staffing becomes an issue that has to be discussed," said Breining. "Either our profit is being eroded or we are in a losing situation. Hopefully, our systems are good enough that we don't get to that in the last minute. There are times when we have chosen to take a lower profit because either the client gives us a lot of business, or we want more business from them or they have done something for us. That's a business or management decision. But up until that point, there are no rules about what they can do with customers."

W Hotel: Don't Bend Customers to Fit the Rules

Because the W Hotel brand is so new, the company is unencumbered by a surfeit of historical rules, policies, and standard operating procedures and policies. The company, of course, has rules that are pertinent to good business in the area that the hotel industry calls "the back of the house"—the operational areas—which include good cash controls, credit card processing, processing of cash vouchers, and so on. "But, beyond that, we are refreshingly absent of rules," enthused Tom Limberg, general manager of W Seattle. "I don't think they're necessary. Good service is not about an employee with his head down looking in the three-ring binder rule of rules. Instead, we want them working with their head up, looking for opportunities to wow someone. It's about tone. We don't live in a world of black and white; we live in a world of gray, where we bend rules to fit customers. We don't bend customers to fit rules. That's what empowerment is."

The absence of rules is evidence that the W Hotel eschews structure and formality. "The basic standard is in place for the guest to be checked in efficiently,"

Thomas Martin, W's corporate Casting Director, told me. "Wrapped around that basic standard is the personality of the individual cast member. We are not rigid. If a guest calls room service for breakfast at one minute after 12 noon, and breakfast stops at noon, we aren't going to say 'no' if the guest asks for eggs. Why should we? We have eggs, we have a cook, and we have a stove. We're going to make the eggs. It's as simple as that."

FirstMerit: Decide What's Best for the Customer

When John Cochran first arrived at FirstMerit Bancorp in 1995, he found an organization that was "very operationally orientated," he recalled. "It wasn't a marketing organization, which is what we are today. FirstMerit had all sorts of clearly stated procedures that were quite severe and radically customer-unfriendly, and there were severe penalties for not following those procedures."

Ever since he assumed the position of chairman and chief executive of FirstMerit, Cochran has tried to eliminate as many rules as possible and to create a company that is "like Nordstrom, where employees are encouraged to use their common sense," he said. That means that employees are allowed to use their good judgment when they evaluate a situation. "For example, if you feel you should waive a charge for a customer because the situation warrants it, go ahead and waive the charge. If you think it's necessary to make an apology for the institution, please do it, because that's what's going to give the customer the best impression for the company. That's what a great marketing company does. The primary question should always be: What is going to be best for the customer? It all goes back to empowering your people to take ownership of the customer situation."

Executive vice president George Paidas felt that FirstMerit has done a good job of overcoming many regulatory roadblocks to customer service. "John Cochran has been a Messiah in the sense that he's relegated the [bottomline] audit function to something other than the leading force in the company. He has taken the department that worries about credit quality and put them in truly a support position, as opposed to a lead position."

In the old days, on the credit side of the business, there was virtually no deviation from the policies and expectations that were laid out by management. If a borrower was faced with an exceptional situation, even if that exception was clearly understood by the frontline loan officer, that officer would have a difficult time convincing his superiors at headquarters that it was in everyone's best interests to restructure the loan. Today, accountability rests at the local level.

FirstMerit has also raised the threshold on the amount of money that can be loaned to a client before that loan has to be approved by the bank's lending committee at its headquarters in Akron, Ohio. "We are able to do much more now on a local basis," said Paidas.

Paidas believes that FirstMerit has no further to go in terms of eliminating rules. Instead, the challenges that the bank faces are issues of how resources are allocated to support areas, such as the Services Division and Consumer Loan Operations, that are not part of the salesforce. "John really has turned this into a marketing organization. If you take the strides we have made on the sales side and compare them to where we are on the service side, we've created somewhat of a gap. The challenge now is to close the gap by allocating resources to service what we've sold," Paidas observed.

St. Charles: Take Charge of the Situation

St. Charles Medical Center in Bend, Oregon, reduced the number of its policies and procedures by about 60 percent, according to chief executive officer Jim Lussier. "For example, we found that the registered nurse at the bedside of the patient was in a situation where she was spending more time shuffling paper and dealing with medical records than she was tending to patients and communicating with family. One of our quality goals was to turn that upside down," said Lussier.

St. Charles combated that situation by instituting a procedure called "exception charting." As Lussier explained:

> *If every time you go into a patient's room to check his vital signs, and you see that those vital signs are within the limits that we think they need to be, they don't need to be charted. We don't want the nurse to spend her time describing how normal the patient's course of recovery is. What we need to chart are the exceptional things that the staff may need to know in order to react to a change in the condition. That one step cut the amount of paper that nurses were involved with by about 50 percent. As a consequence, we reinvested all that time back into clinical direct relationship service. That was a very powerful tool in telling people what we were all about. We were no longer the big medical-record mill that they used to think that we were.*

Over the years, St. Charles has made wholesale changes in process simply by examining every policy and procedure—including examining the historic reason why a policy or procedure was implemented in the first place. "For example," Lussier, recalled, "quite often, we found that seven years ago something happened in the emergency room that had never happened before, and the emergency room supervisor at that time said, 'We need a policy about that.' So, somebody wrote a policy specifically about that particular incident. Years later, although that type of situation never occurred again, the policy was still on the books."

Therefore, St. Charles set about changing the mind-set and philosophy of procedures by empowering its caregivers. "We changed things by telling people: 'You're in charge of the situation. If you guys can stay within these fence lines and use the values of St. Charles, then you make the decisions you need to make. We'll support you every time. You don't need to look into a policy and procedure book about how to do that. Use your best judgment,' " said Lussier.

By trusting people to use their best judgment and telling them not to be dictated by strict policies and procedures, St. Charles has found that "People are willing to crawl out on limbs and make decisions and muddle through a situation that is sometimes life-threatening."

In the process, the folks at St. Charles discovered an amazing thing:

> We found that the quality people—the good, assertive folk that we have always relied on—weren't using all those policies and procedures anyway. In their own minds, they had already dumped the rules and were naturally using their best judgment. We were fooling ourselves that we had that kind of control.

THE WAY OF DEALING WITH RULES

Great customer service companies try to have as few rules as possible because they know that the more rules a company has, the farther and farther the frontline people move away from intimate relationships with the customer. Rules get in the way of empowerment; empowerment gets in the way of rules. They can not coexist peacefully. When it comes to replacing the rules with approaches that foster innovation and empowerment, great companies take these steps:

- Trust the judgment of your frontline workers. If you don't trust them, why did you hire them?

- Re-examine every rule and regulation in your organization. Let each rule stand or fall on its own merits. Do those rules and regulations make sense in today's business environment? If not, dump them!

- Simplify the procedures that your employees use in taking care of the customer.

- Remember what Tom Limberg of W Hotels said: "We live in a world of gray, where we bend rules to fit customers. We don't bend customers to fit rules."

- Do what's right for the customer—and right for the company.

- When in doubt, do what Continental Airlines did: Burn your rule book!

- Promote one main rule: The Golden Rule, whatever that means for your company.

7 Promote Competition

Don't knock your competitors.
By boosting others, you will boost yourself.
A little competition is a good thing
and severe competition is a blessing.
Thank God for competition.

—Jacob Kindleberger

Competition—both external and internal—stokes the competitive fires at Nordstrom and most great customer service companies. Ever since the early 1950s, all Nordstrom employees on the sales floor have earned the lion's share of their compensation from commissions on sales. The company has always believed that its strength was in hiring motivated, competitive people, paying them according to their ability, and encouraging them to build up their businesses to earn even more money.

One of the paradoxes of the Nordstrom system is that, on the one hand, the company insists that every employee be a team player and everyone competes on a level playing field. On the other hand, Nordstrom encourages employees to become star performers, by outproducing their teammates. From as far back as the

173

1930s, the members of the Nordstrom family (all of whom have been intensely involved in all kinds of sports, from tennis to mountain climbing) used sales contests to promote (presumably friendly) rivalry among associates. For example, if the store were overstocked with red pump shoes, Nordstrom would suddenly launch a contest to see who could sell the greatest number of red pump shoes. The winners were lavished with cash, flowers, dinners, or trips. The losers were, well, losers. "In a sense, every day was a contest," Elmer Nordstrom, the son of the company's founder, once told me. "Everyone tried to do their best, so that they wouldn't be stuck at the bottom of the list."

Today, Nordstrom salespeople receive either a base salary of about $10 an hour, or a commission on sales—whichever is greater. The average commission is 6.75 percent, somewhat higher for shoes, cosmetics, and accessories. Salespeople are given a "draw"—an account from which they draw payment against future sales commissions. But if those salespeople are earning only their hourly wage, they won't be in sales for very long at Nordstrom. If they continue to struggle with a mediocre sales performance, they will either be given additional training, moved to a nonsales position, or fired. It's that simple.

Because it constantly stresses the importance of sales, Nordstrom promotes a dynamic tension among its employees. All of them have ready access to sales figures from all departments and stores in the Nordstrom chain, so they can compare their performance with that of their colleagues—whether those colleagues work across the selling floor or across the country. One of the most important performance barometers is sales-per-hour, or SPH, in the Nordstrom vernacular. Each employee's semimonthly sales-per-hour figures are posted clearly in a backroom of the store for everyone to see. You know how I'm doing and I know how you're doing. Needless to say, the bottom of the standings is not where you want to be.

The company rewards outstanding sales-per-hour and sales-per-month performances with cash prizes or trips, awards, and good, old-fashioned public praise for a job well done. "You can't ever miss the opportunity to reinforce, recognize, and reward the behavior," said Nordstrom vice president Jammie Baugh.

The best salespeople attain the designation of "Pacesetter" by meeting or surpassing the net sales volume goal that is set for their specific department for a one-year period. (For example, the annual Pacesetter target in the women's apparel division is $330,000.) Pacesetters are given an event in their honor and a certificate of merit; specially printed business cards identifying them as Pacesetters, and a 33 percent discount credit card (13 percent more than the average employee discount) for one year. A first-year Pacesetter also receives a business-card holder, and assorted baubles, such as an engraved pen or a diamond-and-sapphire lapel pin. The company rewards other top performers with incentives such as cash and gifts, as well as the opportunity to be assigned to the best work-shift schedules, which gives them an opportunity to make additional money.

As you might expect, such an emphasis on selling occasionally leads to excesses. Some salespeople have been known to try to find ways of beating the system or outmaneuvering their fellow employees. But people who do that on a consistent basis don't last very long at Nordstrom. And despite the infrequent cutthroat behavior, Nordstrom's top sales performers wouldn't change the commission-oriented system. "It's not just that you're putting money into the Nordstrom's pocket," said a salesman. "You're putting money into your own pocket."

When individuals and departments have a successful day, or are "on target" in reaching their goals, they are praised by the store manager when he makes the morning announcements over the public address system before the store opens. Monthly store meetings serve as a kind of revival meeting where positive achievements are honored. Letters from appreciative customers are read at these monthly meetings and, at times, over the store intercom.

Goal-setting is an essential competitive tool of the Nordstrom way. All employees involved in sales are continually working to meet daily, weekly, monthly, quarterly, and annual goals for themselves, their department, their store, and their region. Work shifts often start with a reminder of the day's goals; managers frequently quiz sales associates on their personal goals. If a department doesn't reach the goal for the day, a canny manager ups the ante for the next day. Peer pressure and personal commitment push the most competitive employees toward perpetually higher goals.

Just as in the 1930s, Nordstrom uses intercompany competition as a tool for motivating the troops. "We tend to manage by contest," explained Nordstrom executive Jammie Baugh. "When we have something we want to improve on, then we have a contest." Each division in the company runs monthly MNS (Make Nordstrom Special) contests, where good ideas or suggestions are rewarded with cash.

One example of Nordstrom's managing by contest, took place during the fourth quarter of one year, when the company issued a "$250,000 Super Service Challenge." Typical of Nordstrom, there were both individual and team cash awards for outstanding customer service in individual categories, such as timeliness of approach to the customer; and team categories, such as store cleanliness. The judges (who posed as customers) included Nordstrom regional general managers (who were assigned stores outside of their region, so that they wouldn't be recognized), merchandise managers, and employees of an outside professional "mystery" shopping service. To maintain the momentum and excitement throughout the 18-week contest, the company handed out five individual $2,500 cash prizes every two weeks. To be eligible for the drawing, a salesperson had to have received a perfect score from the judges. Twice a month during that 18-week period, at morning meetings before the store opened, the store manager handed out checks for $2,500 to each winning salesperson. "It was like Publisher's Clearinghouse," recalled Baugh. At the end of the contest, a total of $100,000 had been given to 40 top salespeople. An additional $100,000 was given to the store deemed the best for its overall shopping experience. As the employees gathered for their regular morning meeting, a local high school band blared their fight song. Down the escalator came a Nordstrom official with a blown-up check for $100,000.

Clearly internal competition is a controversial topic for American business. Other than FirstMerit Corporation, most of the companies I interviewed had problems with the idea of internal competition, but they all relished the concept of external competition. Typical of that attitude was Richard Kessler of Kessler's Diamond Center in Milwaukee, who told me, "We want to create a team to compete against our competition, not among ourselves. We need to support each other. It's a team effort."

Kessler's salespeople are paid a commission on top of their regular salary, but, unlike many other jewelry stores, Kessler's does not split commissions among its employees "Let's say you work with a customer today, and then you go on vacation next week and that customer comes in and buys a $10,000 ring," said Kessler. "When you return from your vacation, you'll find that commission in your mailbox with a note saying, 'Congratulations, you just made a beautiful sale.' " With a philosophy, like that, Kessler feels that he can outdo his competitors by fielding a solid team of people who are all on the same page.

Competition can take different forms. The Feed the Children charity in Oklahoma City believes that its own brand of competition takes place internally among each individual who works for the greater good of the ministry. "Instead of the competition centering around the idea of 'I beat you this month and you're not going to catch me,' the competition is within each one of us," explained vice president Paul Bigham. "You can sit back and say, 'Look what we as a group accomplished, and I was a part of that. I want to accomplish more, so more children can be fed.' "

Even though theirs is a religious, Christian-based organization, the management of Feed the Children stresses to employees and volunteers alike that the ministry must still be run like a business. "We emphasize to each person: 'You're a professional. Do a good job, and for no other reason, do it for your faith; your higher power,' " Bigham declared.

In the vastly different world of Mike's Carwash, the idea of internal competition is evidenced by the friendly rivalry between the teams at each of Mike's 19 locations. That rivalry can spark improvement for stores and individuals alike.

"Every month, we have a meeting in our central office. One month we'll invite the managers; the next month the assistant managers," described Bill Dahm, president of the family-owned concern. "We project onto a big screen everybody's financial numbers. We go through all the expenses and sales and everybody can see how they're measuring up to the team average, and how they compare to the outstanding stores."

In addition to the raw numbers, every employee at Mike's is rated on customer service by mystery shoppers, who visit the stores each week with a concealed tape recorder and tape the entire experience, including what the employee said to the customer, how a question was answered, and so on. The findings of the written report of the mystery shopper are shared with the people attending team meetings. "We use these tapes to find people who are doing the right things and people who are doing the wrong things," explained Dahm. "If somebody has done something that was not accurate or not according to procedure, we will quietly pull that person aside and explain what they did wrong and how to do it right the next time."

Mike's Carwash has found that by playing and replaying the audiotapes and reviewing and re-reviewing the written reports, the chain has the ideal opportunity "to constantly reinforce the kind of behavior that we're looking for," said Dahm.

Although the W Hotel brand doesn't want its "cast members" to compete against each other, the chain does promote friendly competition among departments, according to Thomas Martin, W Hotel's corporate Casting

Director. "For example, we will single out housekeeping or the restaurant when they do well in a particular month." In addition, Martin pointed out, "There is a lot of competition in our Guest Service Index. J.D. Power [the consumer survey company] does independent audits of all of our guests on a monthly basis. I think it's healthy and we publicize it because that gets the whole team behind it." Martin does add the caveat that competition among W Hotels is sometimes like comparing apples with oranges because of the differences in the various hotel markets and locations.

But as a general manager, Tom Limberg of the W Seattle, enjoys being competitive with the other W Hotels. "Now we're talking team," he said with relish. "We have tremendous competition with W San Francisco, which opened around the same time we did, and is about the same size. We have fun with each other. That's where competition is healthy. People like to win. When you reinforce winning, it's a very contagious growing situation."

USinternetworking promotes internal competition among its Client Assistance Teams or CATs. The competition is based on the standard goals and measurements that the USi, an Application Service Provider, sets for its call centers. For example, there is a contest for the best average speed to answer a call. (The company's target is to answer 85 percent of its calls in 20 seconds or less; 90 percent in less than 30 seconds.) Taking a page out of *The Nordstrom Way,* each month, USi posts the performance statistics within the company for every team member to see. When approached correctly, the standings can become a source of inspiration—for the leaders to stay on top; and for the also-rans to improve. "The CATs are very competitive," said

John Tomljanovic, Vice President of Client Care. "Each one wants to be the best."

Another element of the competitive situation at USi are Client Satisfaction Surveys, which are a factor in how each CAT is rated in serving and satisfying its clients. On an informal basis, the company occasionally hands out spot bonuses for teams that have done an excellent job. These bonuses can include dinner with a spouse at a fine restaurant or tickets for hockey or basketball games.

One of the prime incentive targets for the Client Care group at USinternetworking is a client satisfaction rate of 90 percent or better. Tomljanovic told me:

Everybody in the group—from my team to the people in charge of engineering solutions to the people in deliveries is tied to it. We believe that if you can tie client satisfaction to the compensation of everybody in the company, including the people who are not part of the client care group, you are sending a tremendous message to our clients of how focused we are.

Continental Airlines is a company that has succeeded by joining together to battle its rivals. Gordon Bethune, the chairman and chief executive officer, emphasizes that, "The competition isn't amongst ourselves. The competition is the other teams—American, United, Delta. We give our people tons of metrics on what the competition is doing, and where we stack up. We focus on everyone working together to take care of the passenger. We are a team. A good metaphor is that we are a wristwatch with a lot of parts that function in conjunction with each other. We only work when we all work together. We only win when we all win."

When Bethune took over the then-ailing airline in 1994, he found a company where a series of previous management teams had poisoned the idea of internal competition by playing off employees against each other. "The only way we all win is if we take care of all the baggage and all the seating and take off and land on time. That takes teamwork. The gate agents and the flight attendants work together because they only win when the customers win, which means getting the passengers to their destination on time," said Bethune. "Customers measure success very simply: 'Did I arrive safely and on time and with my underwear?' "

Continental's employees "win" when they place among the top three airlines in on-time arrivals. "'On-time' drives everything," Bethune emphasized. So, they not only have to make sure the planes arrive at their destination on time, they also have to have a performance record that is as good or better than the competition. Competition in the relatively small airline industry is easy to measure because every month, the government publishes the standings—first place through last place—based on on-time performance, number of bags lost, customer complaints, and so on.

When Continental Airlines ranks among the top three performing airlines or its on-time record that month is at least 80 percent (as reported electronically every month by the U.S. Department of Transportation), every employee—manager and below—receives a $65 extra bonus that month. If the airline ranks first, each employee receives $100.

Bethune initiated that bonus program as soon as he took the reins of the company in January 1994, a time when Continental consistently was ranked at the bottom—tenth place. The following month, the airline came in fourth—for the first time in recent history, so every employee received a bonus check. To drive home the point that this bonus was, indeed, something special, Bethune asked the payroll department to issue the bonus on a check that was separate from the paycheck. "You couldn't electronically deposit it. You had to get it and cash it," Bethune recalled. The memo on the check said, simply, "Thank you for helping us be on time in February 1995."

Bethune noted that when employees received those checks, "Everybody was startled because the previous CEO had been trying to figure out how to take money away from them. This was money that was extra; it was not in the contract."

The following month, March 1995, Continental came in first place in on-time performance. "We hadn't been in first place in 60 years. Everybody was stunned," said Bethune. "They got another check. Then in April, we came in first place again. We showed ourselves what we could do when we saw we could compete."

To promote that competitive edge among their employees, many companies find great value in giving out awards and bonuses—both the expected and the unexpected.

Callison Architecture promotes competition within the firm with "a very aggressive bonus program that is based on performance," explained partner Stan Laegreid. Every year, the firm conducts a review of each employee's performance, which ultimately determines the bonus for the year ending, and the salary adjustments for the following year. "We deliberately set up the bonus as a strong incentive program. Our goal for people who have been here at least a year is a top-to-bottom bonus program. If the money is there, there is a bonus for the lowest paid person to the highest paid person. Just as your ability to contribute to the success of the firm grows with time and experience, so does the percentage of your salary that could be bonus-driven. Your salary may get to a point where it flattens out, but you have the chance to continue to enhance how the firm does. So that bonus may progress in percentage. There are no guarantees, but people who have been here a few years see this bonus program as a real incentive."

Cohen's Fashion Optical, a regional chain of eyewear stores, is part of a trend of companies who are grappling with the challenge of attracting and retaining workers, and making them feel good about helping their company compete. Cohen's found a clever way to reward employees who met specific sales goals. Those who hit the marks were awarded points, which could be redeemed for gift certificates at online retailers on the Web site of 800GiftCertificate.com. Robert Cohen, chief executive office of Cohen's Fashion Optical told the *New York Times,* "Employees use points to buy books, dinners—they're all over the place with them." Cohen's 300 employees can log onto the 800GiftCertificate site to track the points they earn toward their incentive awards. To Cohen's, online corporate gift certificates are an inexpensive, hassle-free way to offer employee bonuses for outstanding performance.

At Great Plains Software in Fargo, North Dakota, the company strongly believes in rewarding employees who give outstanding customer service. When a customer writes a letter of commendation to a customer-support representative, that representative receives a bonus. One customer, who had worked regularly—and successfully—with one particular representative, flew that representative and his wife to Chicago, where they were his guests at a Chicago Bears football game. Thanks to those types of rewards, Great Plains employees have returned as many as 249,020 straight calls without missing a customer deadline.

Of all the companies involved in this book, the one that most completely embraces the Nordstrom philosophy of internal competition is FirstMerit Corporation. FirstMerit has created a state-of-the-art system for rewarding internal competition that far surpasses not only Nordstrom, but also any other company that I've ever heard of. That's why the rest of this chapter is devoted to how this bank, based in Akron, Ohio, does it.

"We thrive on internal competition," declared John Cochran, CEO of FirstMerit Corporation. "This organization is very performance-based. Like Nordstrom, it's not for everybody. All of the people who generate sales for FirstMerit are involved in incentive compensation plans, which are a true motivator for many people who have a strong desire to be rewarded in their paycheck."

FirstMerit uses its sales development team to create tools for measuring virtually every aspect of an employee's performance. "Those measurements are a tool that enables our coaches [supervisors] to look not only at the performance of each employee, but also to look beyond the numbers so that we can measure their skill level as well. If there is a skill deficiency, then we will get them more coaching, said Cochran.

In 1995, Cochran brought in Ilene Shapiro to run the bank's sales development department, which is the centerpiece for the processes, procedures, rewards and recognition, incentive programs, and performance-expectations for all areas of the bank. Shapiro's department "conceives, develops, implements, tracks, measures, coaches, and builds incentives and rewards for all of those programs," Cochran explained.

Before FirstMerit introduces a new product or service, the sales development department first helps to prepare and educate the salesforce on what the product is and how to sell it, and then builds internal sales contests around that new product or service. "We try to target the behavior to what we're trying to accomplish. They have to hit specific numbers and criteria, which are all tied to our business plan," said Shapiro.

FirstMerit makes no apologies when it comes to promoting friendly competition among individuals. "We stack-rank them. We measure them. We publish the results," Shapiro elaborated. "Everybody knows what they are competing for. They are watching each other's numbers. There is a healthy competition about going after new business. One person will say to another: 'How many new accounts did you get today? How many dollars did you bring in?' Not only does everybody want to win in their own areas, they want to be the best in the organization."

For example, when FirstMerit launched a new home-equity program, the person in each region who brought in the most new money within a certain time period was awarded an all-expenses-paid, four-day and three-night trip to New York City. Second prize was a night on the town, including two tickets to a play and dinner at a high-end restaurant, complete with a limousine driver.

Within the spirit of competition, FirstMerit likes to develop "a healthy sense of camaraderie, by offering a variety of categories, including 'most improved,' where lots of people can get a chance to win something, said Shapiro. (These contests are separate and apart from each employee's basic incentive plan of goals and performance expectations, which are set at the beginning of each year.) The contests run for specific periods of time, usually six to eight weeks, so they create bursts of energy and focus that generate revenue and build customer relationships that can last all year. "Because these contests run for short periods of time, employees know they need to maximize their efforts because they don't know when the next one is going to come."

How does FirstMerit keep that competition from becoming cutthroat? "We're a relationship bank, so each of our people are relationship managers. Whether they are on the retail side or in the commercial or trust arenas, they maximize the relationships with the customers," said Shapiro. When the bank is introducing new products,

> the most natural thing for employees to do is to offer them to their existing customer base. Maybe they are calling the customer about a home-equity loan, because we know, based on our early discussions, the financial needs of the customer. Then the employees will go to their partners in the organization—people in other areas that they have teamed up with before—and ask for help in looking for the new business. Earning all of our customers' business is a goal of ours.

By forming partnerships with fellow employees, "You are not fighting for the same customer, but rather working together to meet the customers' needs. You are competing for dollars," she added. "There might be some overlap, but, by and large, there's not that much."

FirstMerit's approach to internal competition, "is that we serve the customer at the customer's point of entry. If one branch is more convenient for the customer, we're going to do what's right for the customer. So, we don't have a great deal of fighting over a customer now that our basic philosophy has been ingrained," said Shapiro.

Competition at FirstMerit consists of two parts. The first is competition among individuals because, "You need to understand how professionally you are handling your job," Cochran explained. "So, we stack rank every-body against everybody in terms of performance crite-ria so that every employee knows where he or she stands relative to others in the organization."

But the second part of that equation is that individ-uals have to operate as a team. Consequently, First-Merit, which was inspired by Nordstrom's penchant for contests, launched a contest of its own, called "The Best Branch," which include a variety of criteria, including achieving sales quotas, service quality, community in-volvement, and reports from mystery shoppers. All the categories and criteria are geared toward enhancing the customer experience while meeting performance expectations and revenue goals. Since everyone has a scorecard, all employees know exactly where they stand, "and what they need to do in order to create that unique FirstMerit experience," said Shapiro. "These are team goals for each bank branch; not the goals of individuals."

As Cochran sees it, "At Nordstrom, the guy who is selling shoes needs the guy selling suits to refer him business. At the end of the day, you're going to figure out that, in order to get good at your job, you need to be cooperative with a fellow team member. At FirstMerit, the personal banker needs the teller referring customers to him. Also, the tellers get some of their compensation through [successful] referrals by personal bankers. So, they need to have cooperative personal bankers who will follow up on those referrals. Plus, they have to understand the product line better. You see bankers who have absolutely no management responsibility for other people in their branch cooperatively working, running training sessions to familiarize the tellers with their product, and feeding back to them what their goals are, and how well they are doing against their goals. They soon learn that it's ultimately in their best interest to work with the other people in their branch."

Cochran believes that FirstMerit's best personal bankers are the ones who have the best teamwork inside their branches. "They don't see the goal as 'my' goal, but rather 'our' goal. They look for how to help each other achieve their goals. We constantly drive home the point that the customer's experience in the branch is fully owned by the branch and by every employee who works in the branch. That's teamwork."

From Shapiro's point of view, "Everyone in the branch is aligned so that we can maximize that relationship with the customer. But if the banker is out sick, on vacation, out to lunch, and a customer walks into the bank, the rest of the team takes it upon themselves to make sure the products or services are being delivered to that customer—with highest-quality customer care. That makes it a collective goal. You can't get to that collective goal unless everybody on the team drives the behaviors or demonstrates the behaviors to get there."

The winning branch (generally comprising about a dozen people) receives a four-day, all-expenses paid vacation to Disney World where they spend some time at Disney's customer service school as well as fun free time at the theme park.

This branch competition is set up like a competition heading to the Super Bowl, with each branch organizing its own team. To generate excitement over the program, Shapiro's office sent each branch an invitation that looked like a football, and asked them to create a fun team name and be prepared to shout it.

"Branches came up with names such as the Broadview Heights Bees. They made up cheers. They decorated cars. They had chants and dances. And they were just so excited, it was a thrill to see. The energy behind it," Shapiro recalled. "At that point, they didn't know what they were playing for. We kept it a big secret. We built a lot of momentum by not telling them. We did a series of five rollouts to the five regions, where we told them parts of the contest, but not everything. When we showed them the Mickey ears and hands, and started singing, 'M-I-C' . . . they realized they were playing for Disney World."

Although FirstMerit made the competition fun, beneath the games exists a serious score card that shows how well the bank is positively managing the behavior and motivation of its employees to get positive results.

After the success of the first best branch, the bank has continued it every year. The bank introduces a new competition every quarter where the branches compete against one another, and are stack-ranked by total points on the scorecard. At the end of the quarter, the bank recognizes 5 percent of the branches, all of whom are awarded gift certificates (which are in the shape of a football) for prize catalogs. The top branch of the quarter receives a trophy; cash prizes are split among the employees in the winning branch.

At the end of the third quarter, FirstMerit again stack-ranks the branches involved in the competition by their cumulative scores for the three quarters. Only the top 20 branches are eligible to compete in the final competition for the Disney World trip. Just for gaining entry into the contest, everybody in the branch is awarded shares of FirstMerit stock.

The rest of the company that is not playing in what the company calls its Super Bowl is playing in the "Merit Bowl" to be in the top 5 percent for additional certificates and money. There is also a "most-improved branch" category.

While the final competition is going on, branches are allowed to challenge other branches in friendly side wagers. For example, if one branch gets higher scores from mystery shops than the branch they challenged, the loser cooks breakfast for the winners. "That keeps the friendly fire going," said Shapiro. "There is a healthy respect for branches and people who are doing it well. Other employees want to learn how this branch or person was able to accomplish so much."

FirstMerit is thoroughly convinced that this internal competition works. "What's the worst that could happen?" asks Shapiro. "Everybody wins. Everybody improves and at the end of the day, the customers are more satisfied, and the organization is a healthy environment to work in." To eliminate strife, "An organization needs to understand the value of competition and stay the course. FirstMerit also hands out individual awards called "First Honors," which, like Nordstrom's Pacesetter designation, is intended to single out the top 5 to 10 percent of the people in the organization. At the beginning of the year, certain criteria and goals are set, and the best salespeople accomplish those goals. "First Honors is a way to celebrate our successes," declared John Cochran. "Each day offers us special moments to be noticed: when someone lends a hand to solve a problem, when someone offers a unique solution, and when someone pitches in to meet a deadline. These moments are noticed through thank-you notes, nominations for First Honors awards, and spontaneous personal responses."

Not every one who works for the bank is involved in selling or even dealing with the customer. There is also competition for simply giving wonderful service. Shapiro pointed out, "People strongly respond to a simple thank-you note. You walk throughout the building and you will see those thank-you notes posted. People keep them. On a down day, it's a really nice thing to look at." So, FirstMerit makes sure that it shows appreciation to those people as well. "We want to recognize, in small day-to-day ways, people who are not in on the competition," added Cochran. "Organizations who think that there is only one dynamic and one behavior will reach a segment of their population, but they won't get that 'heart share.' Recognition and reward are important building blocks. We are constantly looking for ways to reward our internal referral program. If I am a data processor, I might not have a goal, but if I refer somebody and they develop a relationship with FirstMerit, I want to be rewarded."

Another competitive/reward element is the "First-Merit Moment," which is designed to acknowledge single acts of extraordinary performance. "If on a particular day, one of my tellers goes outs and helps push somebody's car that is stuck in snow in the parking lot, that might merit a FirstMerit Moment nomination," said Cochran. When an employee is recognized by a fellow employee for great service or a great contribution to the company, that also warrants a FirstMerit Moment. For example, if Employee A was impressed with how

Employee B handled a special project that they were both working on, Employee A would be encouraged to write a note that praises her colleague. "The concept behind FirstMerit Moments is a way to recognize among ourselves the importance and the value of top-quality, consistent experience," Shapiro emphasized.

There's usually not enough time during the week to write those notes, so every year, around Thanksgiving, FirstMerit sets aside one companywide "First Honors Day," where every key manager in the organization gives employees a half-hour within the day to write a thank-you note or a FirstMerit Moment note of praise, or to nominate an employee for a "First In Service" award, which recognizes a pattern of outstanding customer service. All of the honors require employees to fill out forms and give basic information on who they are nominating and why. Although the forms can be filled out on anyone in the organization, Cochran believes that, "The most meaningful ones come from folks who are not even in your reporting line."

After the forms are filled out, they are sent to the manager of the person being nominated. If the manager so chooses, the FirstMerit Moment nomination can be upgraded to a First in Service award. Conducting and reinforcing these programs is a full-time job because an organization must never lose the momentum it has created. "After we build these programs, we look at how we keep them alive throughout the year," said Shapiro. "If you just put the programs out there and don't follow up and reinforce them, they will atrophy."

At the end of the calendar year, FirstMerit gathers up all the service award nominations, and compiles the top-ranked service people in the organization using a sophisticated point-scoring process. Their managers surprise the winners by showing up at their desk to no-tify them. "It's kind of like Publishers Clearinghouse ar-riving at your doorstep," described Shapiro.

FirstMerit then recognizes winners at both local and corporatewide events. It's up to each branch, region, or division to decide how they want to honor their fellow employees. Some regions chose to organize a bowling night or a laser-tag party. Shapiro recalled one dinner in December that was built around a holiday theme. "We spent a great deal of time acknowledging the folks who received nominations in my area. It got very emotional. There were tears shed and standing ovations for people. It was just incredibly moving."

The centerpiece for the year is the corporate cele-bration—a major production where approximately 250 to 300 winners who are selected for First in Sales and First in Service are "treated like royalty along with their guests," said Shapiro. One year, it was held at the Rock 'n Roll Hall of Fame in nearby Cleveland, where the at-tendees were entertained by a band that played 50s-era music. One of the highlights was when CEO John Cochran and other top managers came out dressed as a rock 'n roll band. When the bank rented out the Palace Theatre in Cleveland, Cochran and company performed, in his words, "a banker's ballet" as they moved about the stage. On another occasion, they came out dressed like John Travolta in *Saturday Night Fever.* And one time, FirstMerit rented out Jacobs Field, the home of the Cleveland Indians baseball team, where the winners' faces were flashed up on the mammoth outfield score-board. "These events are designed to say thank you for a heroic performance," said Cochran. "And the people who won appreciate the healthy peer pressure of inter-nal competition."

THE WAY TO BEAT THE COMPETITION

The companies that are most serious about customer service find ways to stimulate the competitive juices of their motivated, empowered employees. Some companies motivate with money; others motivate with praise and recognition; and others use all three of those elements to attract and keep those great employees:

- Find the competitive element that will motivate your employees.
- Find ways to reward those employees.
- Honor your star employees.
- Promote teamwork among groups within your organization and find ways for them to compete—on a positive basis—with other teams within your organization.
- At the same time, promote the larger team your entire organization—in its competition with your rivals.

 **Commit 100 Percent to Customer Service**

*There is nothing so nice as doing well by stealth
and being found out by accident.*
—Charles Lamb

Finally, after all is said and done, the foundation of
every relationship—including, of course, customer service—is commitment; commitment to honesty, to truth,
and to service. In other words, it is the manifestation of
the core values of the company and the people who com-
prise that company.

Theresa Breining, the CEO of Concepts Worldwide,
the San Diego-based meeting planner says that when
pitching a client, she and her colleagues "share what
our values are. In fact, we include our values in the pro-
posals that we submit to our clients. We try to be genuine in our discussions. We share how we work. We
share comments from other customers. Declaring our
values makes a stronger statement about whom we are
and what we believe in and how we're going to take care
of them. This is so much more effective than saying
something banal like, 'We're really good with customer
service.' In some cases, our discussion of values has
had a profound effect on people. The clients, who make

service and ethics and honesty and integrity the building blocks of their culture, they will get it. And those are the companies that we want to work with anyway."

For those reasons, Concepts Worldwide is constantly reinforcing its customer-service values to potential clients. Breining admits that values can be

> *a tough sell because what we sell is intangible. You can look at a dress from Nordstrom and a dress from Kmart and see the obvious differences in quality. You can't do that with meeting planners without experiencing what kind of job the planners have done. So, we have to rely on what other people have said about us. We're not the cheapest in our industry; we will always be underbid. If a client wants to make us a commodity, we don't want that client. But if they want a planner that's committed to taking care of the customer, that's who we want as a client.*

St. Charles Medical Center of Bend, Oregon, is constantly reinforcing to its staff that the health facility is "making service excellence as much of our quality measure as clinical excellence," CEO Jim Lussier told me. "For a long time, health care was solely based on clinical quality and didn't even recognize that customer service helped determine the psychological or social orientation of the patient—or that it was important in clinical care. It is important. To a large extent, it helps determine all that clinical excellence." Lussier and his staff are continually reinforcing the idea of customer service at St. Charles. "We're not bashful about using the word 'customer.' Our competition is not the hospital down the road or some doctor's office. It is the standards that are being set by the Nordstroms and Lands' Ends and Staples of the world. If those companies can achieve those standards, why not us? It is a battle to

get customer service to that level; it's a constant re-
training process for both our own staff as well as the
physicians."

I do a lot of speaking to individual companies, and
occasionally I get a call from a representative of a firm
who declares that "This year, we're emphasizing customer service." That comment begs the questions: What
did you emphasize last year and what will you be emphasizing next year? What I tell those firms is that customer service is not a sometime thing. What makes a
great customer-service company like Nordstrom is its
top-to-bottom, bottom-to-top, day in, day out commitment to providing its customers with great service.

How does Nordstrom do it? One of the ways the company reinforces its values and priorities is through corporate storytelling. Although storytelling became a
popular trend in the 1990s, Nordstrom has been doing
it for most of its century-long existence. At Nordstrom,
these great stories of customer service above-and-
beyond the call of duty are called "heroics," and they
are essential to the corporate culture and folklore because they serve as ready reminders of the level of service that all employees should aspire to. They are simply
the ideal way to pass on a company's cultural values.
Employees who witness a colleague giving great customer service are encouraged to write up a "heroic,"
which describes what happened.

There are many great examples of heroics. One of my
favorites is the story of the customer who made a last-
minute shopping stop at the Nordstrom store in downtown before heading out to Seattle-Tacoma International
Airport to catch a flight. After the customer left the
store, her Nordstrom salesperson discovered the customer's airplane ticket on the counter. The saleswoman
called a representative of the airline and asked if they

could write the customer another ticket at the airport. Have you ever lost an airplane ticket? Of course, the airline said they couldn't reticket the customer. They have rules against that sort of thing. (Remember Chapter 6, Disregard the Rules?) What did the Nordstrom saleswoman do? She jumped into action. She took some money from petty cash, hailed a taxicab, which took her to the airport, where she was able to page the customer and hand her the ticket. That was one appreciative customer. And it's important to remember that the saleswoman, who works on commission, took at least an hour-and-a-half out of her day to do a good deed.

A man who was involved in sales for a scientific supply company wrote the store manager of the Nordstrom store at the Old Orchard Shopping Center in Skokie, Illinois, about a great customer service experience that he wanted to share. The man had an unusual size, 6½ EE, and had been having major problems finding a pair of black wingtip shoes in downtown Chicago, where he lived. At a specialty shoe store downtown near his home, the salesman happily sold him a pair of Florsheim wing tips for $97 and assured the customer that the shoes were the right size. The customer had tried them on hurriedly and bought them. But when he put them on the following day, he immediately sensed that they were not feeling right—and no wonder; they were actually size 7!

"I returned them and informed the store of the mistake and asked if I could get a wingtip in my size," the customer later recalled. "The sales clerk said they didn't stock my size and it would be a special order at an additional cost. I said I don't have the time to wait and would like to return them for a refund on my credit card. The store manager refused the refund and gave me store credit instead. I asked him how could I get store credit if they don't have a shoe in my size? What would I do, buy $97 in socks? So I left angry."

After two days of shopping in countless shoe stores, the man came to the unhappy realization that no one in the city of Chicago carried his size—and it would take two weeks to special order the shoes. Finally, a friend told him about Nordstrom's extensive shoe department, so he drove out to suburban Skokie, where salesman Rich Komie waited on him. Komie measured the man's feet and came back from the stockroom with six pairs of black wingtips, and fully explained the benefits of each type. (See Chapter 1, Provide Your Customers with Choices.)

"I was elated!" wrote the customer, who then told Rich Komie about the treatment he had received at the other store in Chicago. Komie didn't just shake his head to make the customer feel better; no, he called the other store and asked them to refund the customer's money rather than give him a credit, which he couldn't have used anyway. Imagine getting a call from Nordstrom questioning you on your customer service? What else could the salesman from the other store do but give the customer a full refund? The customer ended up buying two pairs of shoes that day from Rich Komie and Nordstrom. "I have never had a more pleasurable experience buying shoes in my life," the customer concluded in a letter to Nordstrom. "Rich even put me in contact with the Nordstrom's tailor for a suit that needed a few adjustments! It didn't end there, Rich even sent me a thank-you card!" After that experience, the man concluded, "I now tell this story to all my new manufacturers representatives that I train and emphasize how total customer satisfaction means not just THE SALE but REPEAT SALES!"

Customer service does not have to be the grand gesture; it can just be a human kindness. "When customers look lost, I will offer them directions," said Len
Kuntz, a Nordstrom executive and former store manager. "When your people see the store manager doing
that, they realize that service is the focus of the company. Much of what happens in this company is envi-
ronmental. You absorb it by watching and seeing the
focus and priorities, and it snowballs."

Xochitl Flores, an employee at one of the Nordstrom
Rack (clearance) stores in Northern California, recalled
the time when her store was closing up for the night and
all of the cash registers were shut down. Before she left,
Flores noticed one credit card payment had accidentally
gone unprocessed. "When I saw that the payment was
due that night, I drove it over to our Stonestown store,
which was still open, so I could make sure the customer
wouldn't receive a finance charge. Because my manager
believes in me, I believe in myself and feel confident to
take on more responsibility instead of doing the same
job and the same tasks every day."

What I like about the story is that Xochitl prevented
something from happening, which the customer never
realized. Let's say Xochitl had decided, "Oh, why bother?
It's not my problem. Somebody will process the bill tomorrow." Then imagine *you* were that customer. You get
your bill from Nordstrom and you notice that there is a
late charge. You think to yourself, "Not only did I pay
that bill on time, I paid it right in the store. How did
Nordstrom screw this up?" Instantly, this customer has
a negative feeling about Nordstrom. But that didn't happen because one empowered employee, inspired by her
employer's (and her coworkers') commitment to customer
service, drove a couple of miles out of her way to save

that customer a late charge. Small gestures count as much as grand gestures.

On a business trip to Seattle, Dr. Charlene Smith from Athens, Ohio, was shopping with Connie Corcoran, a salesperson in downtown Seattle. Dr. Smith had accidentally left her 14-karat gold necklace behind in the fitting room as she hurried off to a convention banquet at a nearby hotel. When Connie Corcoran discovered the necklace, she immediately phoned the hotel trying to locate Dr. Smith. At first, the hotel staff was reluctant to help in the search for Dr. Smith because she wasn't a registered guest. But Connie persisted in insisting they check the banquet roster and find her customer.

Eventually the hotel employee found Dr. Smith at her banquet table and surprised her saying that "A woman from Nordstrom was on the phone" to inform her she had left "something valuable" in the store. Though Charlene Smith had been unaware the necklace was missing, she knew immediately who would be on the phone and why. When Connie arrived in the hotel lobby with the necklace a few minutes later, Dr. Smith ran up and hugged her, thanking her for what she'd done. How many people do you think Dr. Smith told that story to?

That brings us to another key point about the Nordstrom commitment to customer service: Nordstrom has never run an advertisement boasting about its customer service. Nordstrom has never run a press release about a great act of customer service performed by one of their employees. Everything you've heard or read about Nordstrom's customer service has been 100 percent through word-of-mouth. Although these exploits are not shared with the public, they are certainly shared internally within the Nordstrom family in the form of heroics. Frequent recipients of heroics are elected to the weekly VIP Club or selected "Employee of the Month," with their pictures mounted in the Customer Service Room. The week's collection of written-up heroics is circulated among associates. The cumulative effect of this continual reinforcement at Nordstrom is that the front-line workers soon see that the people who run their company single out, honor, and reward outstanding acts of customer service. And those workers quickly learn that the way to advance in the company is to give great customer service.

Continental Airlines: Connect Incentives to Customer Service Excellence

Sometimes that commitment to customer service is fueled by cash bonuses and other incentives. On New Year's Eve of 1999, Continental Airlines wanted to make sure that it didn't have to cancel flights because of a lack of available crews. The holidays are the busiest travel time of year for airlines and, not surprisingly, Continental employees, would rather be at home during that time—especially on New Year's Eve 1999, with all the concerns over the Y2K computer problem. Continental wanted to make sure it was worthwhile for the employees to come to work.

"I said, 'If you come to work on New Year's Eve or New Year's Day, you're going to be eligible for separate drawings,' " recalled Continental's chairman and CEO Gordon Bethune. Eventually, a total of sixty winners were selected in drawings that took place at Continental operations all over the world. Each winner was given a check for $2,000, with Continental paying the income tax, as well. "We also said, 'If you are flying to Paris or Rome or wherever, you, as a working crew member, can take a friend with you. That's normally not allowed." In addition, Continental operations also had New Year's Eve parties and people were given special pins and special recognition for doing a good job.

"Several of our competitors had a huge number of cancellations due to lack of crews," said Bethune. "One of our biggest competitors called us and asked us to share with them how many of our flights were canceled over the holidays for lack of crew members showing up. We said we wouldn't share that with them because we don't believe in sharing that kind of information. But if we had shared it with them, the answer would have been zero, because we cancelled none."

Like Nordstrom, Continental encourages great customer service by implementing profit sharing. Since he took over the airline, Bethune has set aside 15 percent of pretax income on profit sharing over and above salary and bonuses for on-time performance.

"You cannot believe how much of a driver those financial rewards are for people who want to keep the customer satisfied," Bethune told me. "When you run a full airplane as a flight attendant, it's hard work. When you have profit sharing, you are getting extra money for more work. You don't mind doing the work because you are getting some of the rewards of the success. So, it changes your attitude about dealing with huge crowds of customers. Those huge crowds represent your profits. You get part of the pie."

This also holds true for Bethune and his executive team. "I have 20 top people who work for me. Our incentive compensation plan is set up so that if I get incentive pay, they do, too. If I don't get it, they don't get it. Those 20 people will do anything to make sure that I get paid," Bethune said with a laugh.

Mary Kay, the founder of the legendary cosmetics firm, once said, "People respond more to recognition and praise than they do to money and sex." Bethune agreed: "Recognition and praise are the best motivators I know. When you recognize and praise your people, they will go out and do anything for you. Every time you talk to me, you're going to hear me talk about my team and how wonderful they are, and what they did." In his weekly voice mail to all Continental employees, Bethune talks about a variety of topics—upcoming challenges, how the company recovered from a snowstorm, what employees did to help customers get to their destination on time. "Even if we've had a rough week, I'll always brag on our team."

Since 1994, Continental Airlines has published a daily news update—via bulletin boards, e-mail, and voice mail—that passes on industry news as well as a rundown on the carrier's on-time performance and baggage-delivery performance. Electronic billboards from crew break rooms to the executive floor of the lobby in the Houston headquarters are constantly flashing Continental's performance all over the world, because "That's the way we measure customer satisfaction," said Bethune.

Bethune agrees with Nordstrom that customer service must be a top-to-bottom, bottom-to-top commitment. So, part of his job is recognizing great individual performances:

> *Every time a customer writes me and commends an employee, not only will I write back to the customer, I will also handwrite a little note to the employee, underline the nice things that were said, and write thank you. Because we get a lot of nice letters, I do a lot of that—and it pays off. If flight attendants and other employees, who have personal contact with*

customers, receive five such letters, Continental hands out a special star to be worn on their uniform. People know that you are being recognized as someone who gets a lot of accolades.

Bethune frequently gives talks about how to be successful in business. "It's always fun asking people what they think *success* is," said Bethune. "Unless you are going to be a sole practitioner, you are going to have to get people to want to help you be successful. The best way to do that is to openly acknowledge and appreciate them. And when you do that, you get tremendous feedback."

When Bethune is asked how he has been able to run an airline that has been acknowledged for its customer service, he tells them the story of what he and his brothers used to do as kids. "We would find these huge truck tires, bigger than we were," he recalled. "We would drag them out of a muddy ditch on the side of the road, stand them up, which was hard to do, and then get them rolling. If we ran behind them, all we had to do was just hit the tire and it would roll. But if you didn't pay attention, the tire fell back in the ditch, and you had to do all the hard work of getting it back up again. All we're doing right now is running down the road with a big tire. My eye is on the tire. It's not that hard to do, but you better pay attention to the tire."

Feed the Children: Appreciate Your People

At Feed the Children, "Recognition and appreciation are essential. We all want it," said vice president Paul Bigham. "The key is to find appropriate ways to do that. We have general assembly [devotion] times. It's not [officially] a prayer and praise session, but there are times when we will point out above-and-beyond accomplishments. We do that more individually with our departments. In my group, we use what we call show-and-tell in our staff meetings to talk about the great things that our people do for our clients."

If an organization or a small group is unable to come up with the full funding of $5,400 for a full truckload of food, Feed the Children representatives will go above and beyond the call of duty to find another partner or group. "If you've got $2,000, then let's see if we can get another group with $2,000, and we're almost there; let's get the other $1,400. If you're at $5,200, one of our people will say, I'll find the $200 somewhere else from a donor who has discretionary funds, who wants to do this. We'll make it happen; they will get to do their truckload," Bigham promised.

An outstanding example of a heroic at Feed the Children was described in Chapter 4, when a donor representative of the ministry showed up for an appointment at the home of an elderly couple only to find out when she arrived that the husband had died of a heart attack an hour ago. The representative, who over the years had cultivated a relationship with the couple prayed with and comforted the widow while the body was removed from the house. "It's stories like that that drive home the point to our people that we will do whatever it takes to take care of our donors. And that if you take care of the donor, in either a big way or a small way, we will recognize you and praise you for your good works," said Bigham.

Concepts Worldwide: Celebrate Together

At Concepts Worldwide's bimonthly staff meetings, the meeting planning firm "routinely gives acknowledgments to fellow staff members. That is the opportunity for any-body on staff to say thanks for whatever reason," ex-plained Terri Breining. "The successes and the thanks are constantly reinforced because we are highly depen-dent on one another for success, so we need to take the time to say thanks. We have a culture that encourages people to ask for help, and to thank their coworkers when help is given. We also celebrate together. The agenda for staff meetings always include celebrations and ac-knowledgments.

Concepts team members go on two retreats a year, which is part work and part fun. The company might go off to Palm Springs for an overnight stay with a dinner; or stay right in its home base of San Diego where they will spend the entire day in a park on the beach.

Breining says that she commits Concepts to cus-tomer service and employee empowerment by "making it very clear that this is not my company. The success that we've had is really and truly because of the people who work here. They know that I believe that. And that in-spires them to find great new ways to take care of the client."

Callison Architecture: Hear and Relay the Same Message

Like Concepts Worldwide, Callison Architecture uses firm-related functions, such as Christmas parties and spring picnics, to create a family feeling that places cus-tomer service at the center of the firm's raison d'être. Every spring the firm shows employees a "state-of-the-firm" video—how Callison did the previous year, what projects are upcoming; what the firm would like em-ployees to think about. The videos are a convenient way for everyone in the firm to hear the same message.

Also every spring, the company assembles all the employees at one of the main public-assembly projects it has designed in Seattle. Everyone in the office walks over to the project. "That's a way of getting everybody together and communicating," said partner John Bierly. "And at the end of the fiscal year, we have a program where we talk about how we've done. We announce promotions and single out employees for special recognition, which helps develop a feeling of community and helps to motivate people."

FirstMerit: Spread the Tales of Employee Success Stories

FirstMerit uses its First Honors awards, which were explained in the previous chapter, as "important building blocks in creating a strong and lasting tradition of customer service," according to chairman and CEO John Cochran. "We like to recognize each other for positive contributions to our customers on a daily basis through special moments."

FirstMerit has copied Nordstrom's emphasis on heroics. Every week, the bank publishes employee's "success stories" in a weekly newsletter. "These are models of what we want to see done 100 percent of the time in every transaction," said Cochran. As an example of a FirstMerit heroic, Cochran cited the time when a customer was getting his car serviced at a local garage. The customer, who was recovering from a recent operation, suddenly felt ill and asked the owner of the garage to drive him home. The owner said that he didn't have the time to leave his business. So, the customer walked two doors down to his FirstMerit bank and asked the same question of a teller, who shut his window, helped the customer into his car, and drove him home. The customer recovered and is doing fine. The story ended up in the local newspaper. FirstMerit didn't sell that customer a product that day, but they made a customer for life.

The kind of commitment to heroic customer service was in evidence on New Year's Day of 2000. With customers concerned that Y2K might impact the bank's computers, FirstMerit sought to allay their customers fears by having every branch open on January 1—even though it was a holiday. "We told our customers, 'The smart money is in the bank.' And our employees cooperated with us by telling our customers that they could have confidence in FirstMerit because we will be open on January 1 to serve you, and your money will be safe and available to you," said Cochran. And it was.

W Hotel: Make Customer Service Contagious

As a new company, the W Hotel brand is a fascinating case study of creating a customer-centered culture from scratch. As we've said, customer service must be a top-to-bottom, bottom-to-top commitment, and that's what W Hotels is trying to do.

Tom Limberg, general manager of W Seattle, credits Barry Sternlicht, the CEO of parent company Starwood Hotels, with inventing the boutique brand and setting the customer service tone for W Hotels. Guy Hensley, the Starwood vice president in charge of W Hotels has helped create the culture and Thomas Martin, Casting Director, has devised a hiring and training formula that the company hopes will sustain that culture. "Ours is more like a culture in a laboratory than a civilization," said Limberg. "It just grew. Partially by design, luck, and timing, we ended up with a core of people who get 'it.' Today, W Hotels is the strongest culture in our company. That feeling of customer service is contagious."

W Hotels came up with a weekly recognition program for employees who "go out of their way and really and truly show their talent in their role," said Martin. Those employees are given W's Talent Award, which is an acronym for Take Initiative; Always Smile; Listen; Empathize; Never Say No; and Tell the Guest Your Name.

Like many other companies, W Hotels has an employee of the month award, but with a theatrical twist, it's called the "Standing Ovation, which is the ultimate thrill for an actor," Martin pointed out. "Retelling the customer-service story to fellow cast members reinforces the idea of customer service." As an example, Martin cited the story of a businesswoman from the Midwest, who was staying at the W New York on Lexington Avenue and 48th St. "She was very leery about traveling on her own in New York City, and was unable to hail a cab. The guest explained to one of our doormen that she was going to be late for an important meeting and needed to take the subway—something she had never done before. Rather than just point the way to the subway, our cast member walked her to the closest station, took her to the token booth, got her tokens, explained how the system worked, and made sure she was comfortable with what she was doing. Needless to say, she was extremely appreciative."

Interestingly, when this story was repeated in a W Hotel employee training class, someone pointed out that yes, it was a fine story, but what about the fact that the doorman had abandoned his post? The reply to that comment, said Martin, was that "The doorman made sure somebody covered for him at the door. He felt comfortable making that decision because it was his door. He judged the situation, saw that he could manage the situation, and went ahead and did what he thought was right for the customer. For taking a few minutes to help that customer, think of the return on that investment. We're constantly trying to evolve the brand, the hotels, and the employees. Committing to customer service is one important ingredient in that strategy."

Limberg has found that staff meetings, which include the management team, are perfect opportunities to tell stories of great customer service. "It's important that their boss hears about a great example of customer service above and beyond the call of duty. Any note or letter of praise and appreciation from a guest is copied to the employee and placed in their file. I love to walk up to an employee and tell him or her that I just received a great comment about them," said Limberg.

"We're in the memory business, so our challenges are more subtle," said Limberg. "The report card in our business is this: 100 percent is an A; 99 is an F. That's a tough report card."

Mike's Carwash: Answer Every Letter from Customers

"We just happen to wash cars, but the business we're really in is satisfying customers," declared Jerry Dahm, vice president of operations at Mike's Carwash. "We constantly remind our people that the customers make this all possible. We tell them, 'We sign your paychecks, but when the people that you've given good service to come back time and time again, they are making all this possible.' Repeat business is what makes this thing work." Mike's constantly reinforces its commitment to customer service by reading customer comment cards—both good and bad— at employee meetings. And Mike's answers every one of those customer comment cards because part of a company's commitment to customer service is reinforcing that commitment with its customers.

A review of the letters that Mike's receives from customers shows that the vast majority have to do with small but significant things: a broken rearview mirror; scuffs and dullness on the hood and roof; an emblem missing from the front grille of a car. Those things may be small, but when it happens to you, they become significant. In each one of those instances, Mike's made sure the customer received satisfaction, and in virtually every instance, the customer was taken care of without a frontline employee having to ask his or her boss for permission because the employees know they are supported by their management's 100 percent commitment to customer service.

Like Nordstrom, Mike's makes sure that virtually all of the people promoted to positions of responsibility have risen up through the ranks of the company. "We don't get hung up on how long people have been with us. We promote the person who really deserves the promotion," Dahm told me. Those veterans are Mike's best examples of customer service because frontline employees watch what the managers (as well as the owners) do to take care of the customer. "All of our managers are working managers. We don't have offices for them. They are out there setting the example. That's what motivates my people: Seeing that the person running their branch location is doing the same kind of customer relations that we expect out of them."

Realty Executives: Be Accessible and Open with Your Employees and Colleagues

Honesty from the top down is essential to outstanding customer service. Jeff Moore of Realty Executives of

Nevada, feel that he and his wife, Fafie Moore, show their commitment to their independent agents by being "very predictable and consistent as to how we treat people and how we run the business. Every agent knows that they are on an exact parallel with every other agent. We don't cut special deals. Our story is very easy. It's the same story for everyone. Our goal is to provide satisfaction. It starts with the independent contractor and it's conveyed on to the retail consumer. We're accessible to our employees, to the public, to vendors, to agents. Problems don't erupt because somebody couldn't get to somebody to make a decision. The commitment to service is our accessibility and openness, making our home number available to them; calling them back; responding to them when they need help. You can't provide service if you're hiding."

USinternetworking: Don't Be Afraid to Give Atta-Boys

"We're always giving 'atta-boys' when people are doing a good job, because if you reinforce positive behavior, it's going to continue," stated John Tomljanovic, Vice President of Client Care. "Whenever somebody does a good job, either I or the director of that group personally sends out an e-mail, saying thank you, and the whole team sees it. We're constantly sending those messages across the company. Those messages really help our salespeople because when they are out in the field selling to a client, they can tell a story about what somebody in our client care did for a client who was unhappy and how they were able to make that client happy."

USi shows its employees the firm's commitment to customer service by providing explicit data not only on their own company but on the competition as well, through both the Internet and the company's Client Care Intranet Web site. "We provide our people with an incredible library of tools as well as detailed information on the product, services, what our competitors are doing. That information is available to them whenever they want them." Tomljanovic pointed out:

> *Each department has a space on the company Intranet. We put a link out there for every client that we have; the key contacts for that client; what they purchased from USi; who the salespeople were; the experience of the implementation; what phase of work we are in. Anybody in the company can get a feel for how happy or satisfied that client is. We believe that knowledge management is critical for the success of a growing company—to spread knowledge throughout the organization.*

Most of the people hired by USi had previous experience from some of the top software and management-consulting firms in the business, and they are pleasantly surprised at USi's commitment to client service. "When they do execute pursuant to the company strategy, they have an exponential number of very happy customers," said CEO Chris McCleary.

USi's client-service philosophy extends to something as simple—and as important—as phone etiquette. "We believe that phone calls should be returned," McCleary emphasized. "It doesn't matter whether it's a vendor, an employee prospect or job candidate. As a public company, we feel that everybody could be an investor or a client."

It bears repeating one last time that great customer service is in the details; in the simple human kindness. After I gave a speech in Indianapolis to a convention of tour operators, a woman came up to me and said, "I have a Nordstrom story for you, but it's too complicated to tell it to you here." I asked her to send me an e-mail, which, thankfully, she did.

Here is her letter:

In the Fall/Winter of 1992, I accompanied my 33-year-old sister, Cindi, to Seattle where she was to undergo a bone marrow transplant for leukemia. If you've ever seen anyone after they've gone through one of these things, you would think they were in a concentration camp. Skinny, no hair—not even eyebrows, pale, and sickly looking. My sister had an especially hard time and ended up in a wheelchair for a few weeks due to muscle weakness.

After she was discharged from the Fred Hutchinson Cancer Institute, we stayed in Seattle for a few months to keep a constant watch on her progress. At one point, the doctor cleared Cindi to take a few "road trips" to get out of the apartment. Her favorite thing to do was go shopping, so we hauled the wheelchair and my sister to downtown Seattle and ended up in Nordstrom's. Since we are from the East Coast, we had heard of Nordstrom's customer service reputation but never actually visited a store. Picture me wheeling around my sister, pale and sickly looking. (I forgot to mention that my sister was a model and always took pride in her appearance.) Well, most people avoided us because she looked awful! We were going through the cosmetics area of Nordstrom's when a woman from the Estee Lauder counter stepped out in front of us and asked if she could put some makeup on my sister! God love her, I don't know her name, but for one-half hour, my sister felt like a million bucks. This cosmetics saleswoman knew she wouldn't make a sale because my sister looked like she was about to die, but she knew she could make a difference in my sister's last days.

My sister died shortly thereafter, but I will always remember the woman who made her feel like a beautiful human being—knowing she wouldn't make a sale, but she made a difference.

Now that's heroic.

Finally, the best customer service story I've ever heard comes from the annals of Frederick & Nelson, Seattle's grand dame of department stores, which for many years was a division of Marshall Field & Company of Chicago. In the late 1940s, a customer named Katheryn Kavanaugh took her first trip in 20 years to her birthplace in Ireland, where she shot several rolls of color photographs of her aunts and uncles and cousins and of the lush Irish countryside. Upon her return to Seattle, she brought the film to Frederick & Nelson, which sent it off to its film processor in the East. But, somehow, during the rush of the Christmas holiday, somewhere between the store and the film processor, the film was lost. An understandably distraught Mrs. Kavanaugh told William Street, the longtime president of Frederick & Nelson, of her plight. After commiserating with Mrs. Kavanaugh, he asked her for a list and a description of the lost photographs. Then he cabled the list to the Marshall Field buying office in London. There, a buyer hired a local news photographer, who retraced Mrs. Kavanaugh's route through County Limerick, County Kerry, and County Leix and duplicated the pictures she had taken. Mrs. Kavanaugh got her satisfaction.

That heroic tale illustrated Frederick & Nelson's 100 percent commitment to customer service and was a great source of inspiration for employees and customers alike. Frederick & Nelson went out of business in 1992, after 102 years. Today, Frederick's 800,000-square-foot store in downtown Seattle is now the flagship store of—who else?—Nordstrom.

THE COMMITTED WAY

In the Jewish religion, there are 613 commandments. A student once asked a learned rabbi if he could simplify all those commandments for him. The rabbi answered: "The most basic is the Golden Rule; everything else is just commentary."

So it is with customer service. If you strip away everything you've ever read about the topic, you are left with one essential truth: Great customer-service companies got that way because they are committed, with every fiber of their being, to give great customer service. Here is a synthesis of the values and practices that define the Golden Rule:

- Make customer service a core value of your company.
- Reinforce every day that customer service is a core value.
- Always find an opportunity to praise employees for great acts of customer service.
- Recognize and reward those great acts.
- Use financial rewards to encourage customer service.
- Provide your employees with information on how they are doing—and how the competition is doing.
- Make customer service contagious.
- Customer service is the small gesture, the small kindness.
- Celebrate the achievements of your employees.

Index